To Bobbie
a Haddassah heroine

THE HALF-A-DOCTOR

MEMOIRS FROM MY "ASYLUM"

Thank You For your Support to
Haddassah
I hope You will receive many
moments of gleeful enjoyment
+ Laughter from within these pages

HERB SOKOL

Herb Sokol

authorHOUSE®

Sorry for the extra D in
Hadassah

AuthorHouse™
1663 Liberty Drive
Bloomington, IN 47403
www.authorhouse.com
Phone: 1-800-839-8640

First published by AuthorHouse 7/8/2010

ISBN: 978-1-4520-3449-2 (e)
ISBN: 978-1-4520-3448-5 (sc)

Printed in the United States of America
Bloomington, Indiana

This book is printed on acid-free paper.

DISCLAIMER

The events depicted in this book have been recorded as they actually occurred. With the exception of family members and Rosemary Kissel, all the names have been changed.

Today, The Roger Williams Hotel is known as the Hotel Roger Williams and bears no resemblance to the hotel that I managed from 1960 to 1975. In 1996 a new group leased the hotel and invested millions of dollars to renovate the property. Presently, the Hotel Roger Williams is a four-star boutique hotel that is totally unrecognizable from my "asylum."

Contents

Foreword   ix

Preface   xi

The Bumbling Assassin   1

On the Beach - Brighton Beach   5

Sax in the Catskills   7

Prescription For Success   15

The Inn Keeper   25

The Mission   29

Meeting Robert - Room 307   39

The Mafia Caper - Room 307   43

The Naked Couple in the Alley   55

The Seduction - Room 910   59

The Pimp Encounter - Room 617   65

The Friday Partner   69

The .45 Caliber   71

He Punched Me - Room 710   75

Mr. Bierman's Lover - Room 1118   79

The Lady in the Shroud - Room 1001   83

Date with the Governor - Room 1407   87

The Fat Lady in the Tub - Room 1407   91

Fire On The 14th Floor - Room 1407   95

Benevolent Man Of The Cloth - Room 209   97

Witness For The Prosecution   103

Naïvety 201   109

The Water Tank   115

Murder at the Roger Williams Hotel   123

The Voluptuous Blond - Room 208   129

Diversification   135
New York World's Fair - 1964 to 1965   143
Coitus Non-Interuptus - Room 604   147
Barefoot in the Lobby - Room 1002   149
My Neighbor's Indiscretion - Room 207   153
Is It Hard To Change A Bulb? - Room 708   155
Fun in the Dark   157
The Invaders - Room 1011   163
The Philandering Doctor - Room 1204   167
Scratch Me, Scratch Me - Room 1018   171
The Pixie Who Couldn't Fly - Room 1404   175
Cultural Differences   179
The Asylum Is Filling Up - 10th Floor   183
The Invention - 10th Floor   187
The Detective Confronts Radiation - 10th Floor   193
Destruction By Radiation - 10th Floor   201
The Aluminum Pan Mummy - 10th Floor   205
The Start of my New Beginning   209
Magic Fingers - Room 707   213
Crisis Management   215
Moon Over Manhattan   219
The Television Repairman - Room 610   225
The New Beginning   229
The Contractor   235
Epilogue   243

TRUE CONFESSIONS OF A
KIND MAN IN AN ODD PLACE

Growing up my mother, sister, brother and I would anxiously wait for my father to come home from Manhattan each night, so we could sit down to dinner as a family and share the days' experiences. This family time was of great importance to my parents. We would share stories about schoolwork, cheerleading, tennis games, and friends. Conversations you would probably find repeated if you walked into any other kitchen in the neighborhood around that same time.

However, what you wouldn't find in those other households was my father's engaging stories of his days spent as the manager of The Roger Williams Hotel. This was a moderately priced hotel in midtown Manhattan that catered to an unusual combination of local art students, business executives from the neighboring furniture and lingerie industries, tourists, as well as weekly and monthly residents.

The stories I've heard repeated over and over through the years, tell of his daily experiences with the slightly neurotic to the very psychotic. Many people who needed a great deal of attention and assistance sought to satisfy those needs through their interactions with my father. Although my psychology background tells me that these people needed more serious attention, and I'd like to believe that they received it, my father did what he could for them during their stay at The Roger Williams Hotel.

Now I am the last person to seek humor at the expense of other people's troubles. However the images of my father, a kind man just looking to get through the day the best way he knew how and having been naively thrown into some of the most bizarre situations, just had to be put down on paper. I hope that the reader can appreciate the absurdity that sometimes is life, as told by my father while sitting around the dinner table.

Jodi L. Sokol

PREFACE

For more than thirty years I have told these stories to family and friends, and always at the end of the tales, I have been urged to write a book. I am quite comfortable being a raconteur and recognized the difficulty in transferring a verbal accounting into a written form that would have the same impact, especially since I tend to write as I speak in a Brooklyneze, Yiddish phraseology. I finally succumbed to the forceful encouragement from my dear wife, Annette, and decided to take on this formidable challenge.

To Annette I say thank you for your support, for the days/weeks and late hours that you invested in editing and untangling my lengthy sentences, and for helping me capture the essence of each event. Without your help, there certainly would be no book. Thank you also for your great innovative camera work that added a unique dimension to the book.

I would like to thank my daughter, Jodi Sokol, who fifteen years ago wrote the Foreword to a book that I finally started writing two years ago. Yes, family and friends have been encouraging me to write this book for a very long time. I finally decided that it was time to put these stories down in print so all my grandchildren can enjoy them (when they are old enough).

Thank you to my grandson, Jason Tarricone for posing as "The Detective" and to my grandson, Jeremy Sokol for posing for what I call "The Naked Boy Jumping Out the Window".

Acknowledgements also go to my daughter-in-law Audrey Sokol, my grandson Jason Tarricone, and to my friends, Barbara Ganick, Barbara Moskowitz, Robin Rosenberg, and Irene Suss who offered to read and edit my first draft copy. Thank you Bob Nessel for your support and encouragement.

Speaking of Bob, Dr. Nessel is among a group of friends that somehow imply that my stories are the gift of a creative imagination ... however, I have yet to meet an individual with a more bizarre career activity than this good doctor. While working for an animal health corporation one of his duties, albeit not a full time activity, was to **masturbate roosters. Not even in "my asylum" could I top this.**

No direct action

or inaction

could derail my navigation

through this vortex called life.

Herb Sokol

THE BUMBLING ASSASSIN

The dark, narrow alley between the church and the hotel partially shielded him from view. The man looked chilled to the bone as he stood there in the rain. He wore a shabby-looking black London Fog raincoat that had definitely seen better days. The collar of his coat was turned up and both of his hands were buried deep in his pockets.

He glanced furtively down East 31st Street with the air of a man on a mission. With each passing vehicle he would quickly retreat into the alley and emerge again only when he thought it was safe.

* * *

I left the hotel at 6:30 P.M. and began walking toward my car that was parked three blocks east at the Red Ball Garage. As I reached the alley I felt an arm grab me tightly around the neck. Then I felt a sharp, pointed object pressing against my throat. I could hear heavy breathing but not a word was spoken. The person did not ask for money and did not threaten me in any way. Nevertheless, I definitely felt I was in imminent danger of a quick thrust that would sever my jugular.

We stayed in this embrace for what seemed like an eternity. I started to wonder—is this person a mugger-in-training who forgot step two, a deaf mute who is locked in silence, or an assassin who is waiting for further direction? Given the desperateness of the situation I figured that I had nothing to lose. I reached into my coat pocket, pulled out my Berretta, and shot it into the air. The mugger/mute/assassin was so startled that he dropped his knife and fled.

Incoherent thoughts started to race through my mind as I stood there in a state of stupor—my entire body shaking. Flashbacks of other frightening events came to mind and then I started to recall how I had come to arm myself in the first place.

As General Manager of The Roger Williams Hotel, I carried cash receipts to the bank and in addition, had other responsibilities that were justification for getting a license to carry a concealed weapon. In a quiet moment of reflection and rationalization, however, I recognized that getting a gun might be a recipe for disaster. Given that I am vertically challenged, when standing erect I measure in at 5'5", a handgun would add 10" to my stature. Chances are that if I possessed a gun, instead of backing away from controversy, I might react too hastily. I feared that I would either hurt some innocent person or get myself killed.

I'm really not sure what I was thinking the day I ordered my .22 Caliber Tear Gas gun from a mail order catalogue. It looked like a Berretta but only fired blanks and/or tear gas pellets. Buying a tear gas gun was probably a foolish compromise because I knew that I could never pull it against a real weapon. I truly believed it would remain in my pocket forever. Forever lasted until this evening!

I continued standing there in the rain until my body finally stopped shaking and my legs felt sturdy enough to walk. Then I slowly proceeded back into the hotel while thinking ... **what the hell am I doing here?**

ON THE BEACH - BRIGHTON BEACH

Born to hard-working Eastern-European Jewish immigrants, I grew up in the Jewish ghetto of Brighton Beach. My father was 5'2" short and a little overweight. He was a jolly and fun-loving kosher butcher, who had a strong tenor voice and aspirations of one day leaving the exciting world of trimming fat off rib steaks and becoming a classical opera singer. The closest he got to this dream was singing in a choir for the Jewish High Holidays.

My mother was at most 4'10", thin, and had black hair. I was probably married by the time I found out that her hair color came from a bottle. She helped my father in the "Progressive Meat Market" most of the day and then walked two blocks from Brighton Beach Avenue to where we lived at 3031 Brighton 13th Street. Mom would then prepare dinner, take care of various household chores, and spend quality time with my two sisters, Carol and Irene, and me

I was a typical Brooklyn boy. My interests were sports, sports and more sports with a little music thrown in for diversification. When I was six years old, my father brought home a violin for me. For the next six years, I struggled with not only the boredom of practice, but also the taunts of my peers. After all, this was Brooklyn! It was embarrassing to walk on the streets carrying a fiddle, to get the lessons that my parents struggled financially to provide for me. All my buddies blew trumpets and reed instruments—the macho instruments at that time.

Sometime around my twelfth birthday, I rebelled! Gathering my accumulated Chanukah "gelt" (money), I took the Coney Island Avenue trolley to Kings Highway and proceeded to rent an alto saxophone from Pearlman's Music Store. To this day it amazes me that this store rented a sax to a twelve-year old, without getting a security deposit or having a parent present. I then became a *closet* saxophone player since I was afraid of my parents' reactions. I knew they would be very disappointed because their dream was for me to become a concert violinist.

Our family lived in a third-floor walk-up apartment facing an inner courtyard and even though our neighbors must have heard the screeches being emitted from my treasured horn, fortunately for me, no one complained to my parents. Since both my Mom and Dad worked in the butcher shop most of the day, I was afforded the time and opportunity (after school) to teach myself this wonderful, pride-restoring instrument.

After one year I felt proficient enough to expose my musical deceit to my parents and friends, as well as to join the Musicians' Union. On the day I auditioned for membership, however, I lost my confidence and ended up playing the violin. But, I made it—**I was now a proud member of the Local 802 Union**.

SAX IN THE CATSKILLS

When I was fifteen years of age *my four-piece band* landed its first summer job. Fortunately for me, my father knew the owner of a small hotel called Lakeside Crest House in Ulster Heights. For those of you who are not from New York, Ulster Heights is a mountainous area outside of Ellenville in the Catskill Mountains and is 90 miles northwest of New York City and 90 miles southwest of Albany.

My band was hired sight unseen and sound unheard. All that they required was a band that could make some noise and play some 'freilachs" (upbeat Jewish songs).

I was the saxophonist and the bandleader. The band also had two guitar players and a drummer. I don't remember how I managed to put this band together but I do remember that the other guys were all older than I was.

I experienced the obvious advantages of being a summer musician in a resort hotel; admiring, young teenage girls would always surround me, well ... maybe one or two. Being a musician in the Lakeside Crest House also had another advantage. The guests enjoyed dancing and/or singing to our music so much that they ended up exhausted and usually left the casino around 9:30 PM.

This early hour gave my band members and me plenty of time to roam the casinos of the larger neighboring hotels such as The Tamarack Lodge and Browns. It didn't take long to realize that a car would greatly enhance our roaming capabilities; so one day I asked Oscar, the Kitchen Manager, if he could give me a lift on one of his trips into Ellenville.

"Sure." he said. "I'll let you know the next time I go into town."

A few days later as I sat in his truck I offered, "I want to check out the junkyard and see if they have a car I can buy."

Not only did Oscar agree to drive me, he even went past his destination and dropped me off me at the junkyard on the other side of the village. Walking into the junkyard I looked around but only saw parts of cars all over the yard. I politely asked the manager if there were any vehicles that had not been stripped yet and were still operable.

He walked me to the back of the lot and pointed to a gray car and said, "That one was just driven in."

"What do you want for it?"

"Fifteen," he said barely looking up at me.

"Could you make it ten?"

"Look the price is fifteen," he replied adamantly.

I got the feeling he thought I couldn't afford it. It was obvious to me it was a deal or no deal situation so I gave the man fifteen dollars and began to wonder if he was truly the manager of the yard or perhaps just some vagrant hanging out. However, that was not my concern. I was now the proud owner, though not officially recognized by the State of New York, of a 1936 gray Buick convertible with a rumble seat. Considering that I had just purchased a car without having a driver's license and without getting a vehicle registration I would have to assume the motor vehicle laws were not strictly enforced in the Catskills in 1948.

I quickly learned that my *new car* had some minor mechanical concerns, i.e.; the auto had a liquid deficiency problem causing it to run out of coolant, brake fluid, and oil every three days. To avoid major inconveniences I kept an inventory of these liquids in the small trunk. In addition, the starter motor burnt out within a day. Now my band members had to push the car until it would start! I soon found it more convenient and practical to seek out parking spaces on an incline thus facilitating a solo moving start.

As I mentioned earlier, the band primarily played upbeat, well-known Jewish music. However, for my own amusement, I would intersperse renditions of current pop favorites. One of these was "Tenderly." I may not have had great technical dexterity on the sax, but I certainly was able to generate one sweet sound.

One admirer of my "Tenderly" was a sixteen-year-old girl whose family rented a cottage about a mile down the road. My *groupie of one* could not be described as especially attractive, but it would certainly be hard to miss her abundant physical attributes. Her name was Cynthia and she made the first overture.

One night, after we had finished our last set, Cynthia asked, "Do you think we could hang out together?"

"Sure. What do you have in mind?" I answered matter-of-factly. But, truthfully, hidden behind this cool response were feelings of excitement as well as nervousness.

"Why don't we walk down to the lake and spend some time on the beach?" she suggested.

"Cynthia, we don't have to walk, I have a car."

So the two of us walked hand in hand to my car and when she saw it she exclaimed, "Herby, can I sit in the *rumble seat?*"

Personally, I couldn't care less where she sat; all I cared about was the hot passionate evening I was envisioning. When we got near the beach I parked on top of a hill, as I had gotten into the habit of doing, and then took a blanket out of the trunk. Even though I was never a boy scout—I was always prepared.

The two of us then proceeded down the path and onto the beach. We stretched the blanket out on what was unfortunately a very rough, pebbly, uncomfortable surface, and proceeded to lie down. Then both of us stared up at the truly magnificent, starry, night sky. After about fifteen minutes of star gazing, I made the first move by putting my arm around her. She was very responsive causing my *anticipation level* to rise. We started to kiss but before long I heard the **thump, thump, thump** of heavy footsteps coming down the path toward the beach.

As the person neared, a deep male voice rang out, "**Cynthia, are you there again?**"

Cynthia jumped up in alarm and with a shudder said, "Uh oh, it's my brother!"

Leaving me without a departing word, she quickly ran to him. In the darkness, I could hardly make him out but he definitely looked huge, very huge, in every direction. In hindsight, I'm happy he wasn't interested in hearing my unique version of "Tenderly."

Cynthia returned to my casino a week later and once again waited for us to finish the last set. This time she invited me to her home. With great expectations I drove toward the cottage while Cynthia enjoyed the evening breezes in the rumble seat. Of course, I took the precaution of parking the car on a nearby hill, which was about a two-block distance from her place. We quickly walked to her parent's two-story summer cottage. It was dark and quiet. Good, I thought, there appeared to be no one at home. She immediately led me up the stairs to her bedroom. This time there was no pretense or delay.

As we entered her room she embraced me, kissed me, and whispered, "Take off your clothes, I'll join you in a minute."

Being self-conscious I hesitated for a moment ... but since the room was dark, I obediently did as requested and jumped under the covers of the twin bed. Cynthia joined me in what seemed like a minute and I was hot and primed. She had also taken off her clothes. I knew this because I could feel her ample breasts pressing against my bare chest as we kissed. Within a few minutes I heard a strange muffled sound that seemed to be coming from the other side of the room.

I was startled and stammered, "Wha ... what is that?"

"It's okay, don't worry. It's only Miriam, my future sister-in-law. We share this room."

My excited state of arousal quickly dissipated. I must admit that Cynthia tried hard to resurrect my previous condition but it was to no avail.

Frustrated, she threw off the covers and angrily said, "Go join Miriam!"

I thought she was kidding. Suddenly Miriam also threw off her blanket and motioned for me to join her. By now my eyes had adjusted to the darkness and I could not believe what I was viewing. Here in front of me was one of the most beautiful young women I had ever seen. I guessed she was about eighteen years old. How lucky could I, a mere fifteen-year-old pseudo-musician, get? To say this was a surreal situation would be a gross understatement. Perhaps I was dreaming.

I jumped into her bed and was enthusiastically welcomed into her arms. My previous *high anticipation level* quickly returned. We barely got beyond a kiss or two when we heard the crunching sound of a car on the gravel driveway.

"Oh, my God, it's my brother!" screamed Cynthia.

"Oh, my God, it's your brother!" yelled frantic Miriam.

Oh, my God, it's your **huge** brother, thought terrified Herby. The two naked girls quickly gathered my discarded clothes, opened the bedroom window, and in a state of panic proceeded to shove my clothes and me out the second story window.

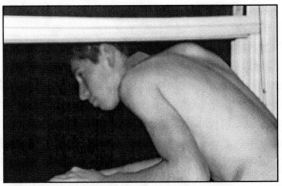

Luckily there was a ledge outside the window. I stood there, looked around, and tried to decide what to do. But I had no choice—I threw my belongings to the ground and quickly followed them down. Grabbing my things I ran for my life—naked, panting, and clasping my clothes close to me like a handy fig leaf.

It seemed like forever until I finally reached my car perched high up on the hill. Without a moment's hesitation I jumped into the car and released the brake. As the car picked up speed, while rolling down the hill, I released the clutch. I heaved a big sigh of relief as the engine caught and I literally and gratefully escaped with my skin intact and my *anticipation level* down to normal. I did not play "Tenderly" again for the balance of the summer.

When I left Brighton Beach for a summer in the Catskills I was looking forward to meeting new people and having exciting experiences. I certainly did both. Socially, however, I found Ellenville to be the same ethnic cocoon as Brighton Beach and I felt like I was suffocating in this tightly wrapped, insulated, social environment which I foresaw no way of breaking out of.

Nevertheless, this summer season was far better than I ever anticipated. Actually it evolved into one of my best. At summer's end, with one of my older band members, I drove my car from Ellenville, through New Jersey, through the Lincoln Tunnel, and into Manhattan. After parking on a nearby isolated street, I bid farewell to my beloved 1936 Buick convertible and thanked it for helping me to have such a wonderful summer.

PRESCRIPTION FOR SUCCESS

Three years later I was accepted into Fordham University's College of Pharmacy. Finally, I was out of the ghetto and in a Jesuit school (of all places) striving for a degree in pharmacy. This degree, I hoped, would present successful entrepreneurial opportunities for my future and, in addition, allow me the exposure to a more diversified environment once I was out in the real world. My four years at Fordham went fast. My grades were good in spite of the fact that I felt like I was sleepwalking through the tough science curriculum.

Looking back I can recollect only two memorable incidents while in college. The first one occurred in my Pharmacology lecture hall. Our professor, though a very bright man, was rather inarticulate and probably suffered from a severe inferiority complex. He would alternate between reading and orating but always with his head down. He would never dare to look up for fear of catching the glance of a student. Well, some proactive classmates decided it was time to help him overcome this inhibition.

One morning they arrived early to class carrying a skeleton borrowed from our Anatomy lab. They strategically placed *Henry* high up in the stadium seating of the lecture hall and placed a newspaper in his bony hands. Of course the professor would not see *Henry* since no glance from him would ever be cast upward.

After the lecture began, one and then two provocateurs seated alongside *Henry* started quietly saying, "**tss-tss**."

Then they kept increasing their volume as they repeated, "**tss-tss, tss-tss**".

The professor's face turned crimson, and then beet red, as he struggled with his dilemma.

From his familiar *eyes to the floor* position he asked loudly, "Who is making that noise?"

The students ignored him and continued with their taunting chant. They kept raising the volume, waiting for the professor to either react or explode from all his built up tension—and react he did. Lifting his head, probably for the first time in years, he noticed *Henry* reading the newspaper.

"Put that paper down and stop that noise!"

Even if *Henry* had wanted to, he did not have the muscle coordination to comply.

"**Stop! Stop!**" And then mustering up all his courage, the professor leapt from the lecture platform and bounded up the stairs to the insolent student. As he grabbed the newspaper he started to scream, "**Didn't you hear me?**"

He stood facing the exposed skeleton for what seemed like an eternity, staring and making eye contact with *Henry's* empty sockets. Then he quietly proceeded down the stairs to the lecture platform where he continued the lecture in his normal manner ... staring at his toes.

* * *

The second incident was actually more embarrassing than humorous and certainly had impact on my future life. I started Fordham University in the fall of 1951, a year that saw the U.S. fully embroiled in the Korean War. The U.S., together with the United Nations, intervened between the North and South conflict in June 1950. To ensure that my education would not be interrupted by the draft, I enrolled in ROTC. Wearing World War II uniforms and firing M-1s on the firing range, brought out a strong sense of national pride in me. I became gung-ho and looked forward to this on-campus activity.

I was even more excited when we were informed that on St. Patrick's Day our ROTC Transportation Unit would parade down Fifth Avenue, with other college groups, and that the procession would be televised. I cannot find adequate words to describe my feelings of honor and elation when we got our "eyes right" command upon approaching the Mayor's reviewing stand. I wished this feeling could last forever. But, of course, most good things ultimately end. However, there is always next year and I couldn't wait to again savor this wonderful feeling.

St. Patrick's Day 1952 came quickly enough and I recall gathering the equipment for my second parade with great eagerness. We started marching down Fifth Avenue, as we had the previous year, and it was just as exhilarating. As we approached the Mayor's stand, my fellow *Second Lieutenants in the Bud* and I got the "eyes right" command and all complied except for **one**. Unfortunately, this individual (no, it was not me) was in our front line. As he started to respond to the command—he dropped his M-1. Need I say more? As he stooped to retrieve it, I think you can imagine the chaos that followed. Each ROTC cadet stumbled over the man in front of him; it was falling dominoes—right in front of Mayor Vincent Impellitteri and on television to boot.

Second Lieutenants were high on the casualty list in Korea and if this performance was to be carried over to the battlefield, I feared that my chances of survival would be pretty low. Upon returning to campus I immediately resigned from ROTC. The Korean War ended the following year in July 1953. Although the draft remained in place and I was subject to it until the age of 35, I never received a call from them. Perhaps they thought I was the cadet that dropped the weapon.

* * *

Upon graduation I looked forward to finally going out into the world, meeting people of different cultures and mingling with professional and intellectual individuals. To my dismay, my world ended up being in neighborhood drugstores, talking to the same people day in and day out, and listening to their "kvetching" over and over. I found I was reaching the point of total frustration.

In the mornings I would open a pharmacy in Greenpoint and in the afternoon drive out to another neighborhood store in Forest Hills where I would work until closing. The geography was different but the issues and problems I faced were the same. If I had ownership in these ventures there would at least have been the challenges, and hopefully rewards, of growing profits. I was getting bored and yearned to be back in the schoolyard of P.S. 225 playing softball, or stickball against the wall, or better yet playing touch football on the warm, soft sand at the beach.

My cousin, Bernie Siegel, was one of my classmates in Fordham. He and his brother-in-law were fortunate enough to be able to raise financing and open a pharmacy in Forest Hills, Queens. Their store was about one mile from the one in which I worked. In October 1960 fate played its hand; Bernie called and described his plight. His partner had taken ill and would no longer be able to work in the pharmacy.

Enthusiastically, he described his wonderful business. Bernie offered me the opportunity to purchase part ownership in his thriving drugstore in Forest Hills, Queens. However, in my mind, I pictured being trapped having to talk to and placate middle-class *yentas* forever.

For example: in the Forest Hills store that I was working in, one woman actually had the nerve to call and ask for delivery of a small bottle of aspirin, "and since you're coming up anyway could you be so kind and pick me up the *New York Times* from the luncheonette next door?" Another woman offered me sex in exchange for some Miltown. I honestly did not think that I could last in this environment for the rest of my working days. More likely, I would be spared because I *too* would undoubtedly become ill and have to leave.

Another opportunity came completely out of left field. My father-in-law had successfully progressed from butcher to photographer to *Hotel Magnate*.

* * *

Sorry! I just realized I went a little ahead of myself and almost missed the most important part of my life. During my college years I dated many but never met anyone that would prove to be of any significance. Perhaps I didn't allow myself to get deeply involved in a meaningful relationship because I feared that it might deter me from my entrepreneurial goals. On the other hand, I knew my mom was concerned that her first-born would never leave the nest and give her grandchildren.

My immediate family consisted of my mom Bella, my dad Julius, and as I mentioned earlier my two sisters. Carol is five years younger and Irene is eight years younger than I am. We were a tight-knit family that survived growing up together in a cramped three-room apartment. So tightly-knit were we, that I shared a bedroom with my sisters until I was sixteen. My parents were forced to use the living room for their bedroom. But our lifestyle was that of many typical, *affluent* Brooklyn families.

Given the age disparity between my sisters and me, our circle of friends was miles apart. And then it happened! My sister Carol accidentally dropped her wallet on the kitchen floor. As I bent down to retrieve it for her, I noticed a photograph that had fallen out.

"Who is this?"

"Oh, that's Annette, a Sigma Iota Phi friend," she answered.

"How come I have never seen her?"

"Because Annette is a sorority member from Madison High School. You've only seen my friends that live around here ... the ones from Lincoln High."

To me it did not matter if she was from another continent, I simply had to meet this girl! One of my favorite female movie stars of that period was Jennifer Jones. The girl in the photograph could have been her clone since they were both beautiful with high cheekbones and Eurasian eyes. To this day Annette still insists that her father, Hymie, during his sojourn in life as a photographer, enhanced her looks by using his excellent skills as a retoucher. The rest of the story is obvious. We met, married, had three wonderful children, Sharyn, Jodi and David and just celebrated our fifty-second anniversary.

I never considered myself a fatalist, but when certain events occur by chance one has to reconsider the concept. Perhaps our life is preordained and no matter what paths we try to take, ultimately, we will find ourselves in the pre-chosen one.

Another strange occurrence took place at our engagement party but let's start this story at its beginning. My future mother-in-law, Shayne Sara (Sylvia), along with her parents, Shifra and Yosel (Sophie and Joseph) Rimland came to America from Poland in 1929. It was an unusually long trip because parts of the Atlantic Ocean froze and the ship was often at a standstill. On this long voyage Sylvia befriended and bonded with two lovely sisters that were about her age.

After arriving in America, she often thought about her ship-friends and wondered what had happened to them. Twenty-nine years later, Sylvia unexpectedly and joyfully was reunited with Eshka (Essie) and Shushka (Shirley), my aunts, at Annette's and my engagement party. My aunts and my grandparents, Leiba and David

Sokol, came to America on the same ship as Annette's mother and grandparents. A coincidence?

* * *

Now we can return to my second business opportunity. My father-in-law, Hyman Rosen, invested and worked with a group of entrepreneurs that took long-term lease positions in rooming houses and west side Manhattan single-room occupancy hotels. For a small investment, one could acquire the title Hotel General Manager and perhaps get a small return on his investment as well.

The reality was the investment group needed a responsible person who, in addition to investing money, was willing to put in the work effort of two or three employees, and was also capable of enduring hard labor such as: schlepping mattresses and furniture, and fixing toilets and refrigerators. Of course, I did not learn about this side of the equation until much later.

This hotel investment possibility was presented to me at the same time that the pharmacy opportunity arose. My father-in-law's group had negotiated a thirty-five year fixed cost lease on The Roger Williams Hotel, a mid-town Manhattan establishment. He was positive that upon introducing me to his investment colleagues they would accept my credentials to run this 216-room hotel on Madison Avenue. After all, how far removed is compounding prescriptions from welcoming and selling hotel rooms to business executives? Obviously it was a perfect match. Remember that term *business executives.*

From my point of view I now had a ten-month-old daughter, Sharyn, and the prospects of additional income and perhaps additional investment dividends looked extremely attractive. I would also have better working hours, which was a definite plus. In the pharmacy I would have to alternate working until 10 P.M. every other night and also alternate working full weekends with Bernie. At the hotel I would only have to work until about 6 P.M. Sunday through Friday and have every Saturday off.

This sounded great to both Annette and me. I could be home for dinner at a decent hour every night and we could make plans to go out with friends and/or relatives on Saturday nights. I would never have to work another Saturday! Opportunity had knocked at my door and I again was envisioning executives, internationalists, diplomats, etc. entering and enriching my life. Annette and I both agreed that this was the brass ring to grasp hold of.

On the other hand, devastation is the only way to describe my mother's reaction when I told her about my decision to become a Hotel Magnate. She looked stunned and then proceeded to cry hysterically.

"After all," she said while sobbing, "**You are half-a-doctor**! How could you leave such a wonderful profession?"

I guess it is every Jewish mother's dream to have a *son the doctor*. Nevertheless, given that I was only half-a-doctor, it was an easy decision for me to make.

THE INN KEEPER

It was 8 A.M. on a delightful "Indian Summer" morning in November 1960. I stood on East 31st Street just off Madison Avenue, in New York City, witnessing sidewalks and roads that were already heavy with both rushing pedestrian and noisy motor traffic.

Looking up, I saw the gold letters Roger Williams Hotel glistening with its reflection of the sun. The hotel was built in 1931 just two years before I was born. The sixteen-story brick structure, however, looked to me as if it was practically new. I could have stood outside all day just taking in this beautiful weather, yet my heart was pounding with excitement and anticipation ... I couldn't wait to start my new career. Fighting my mixed emotions I forced myself to move forward; I entered through the glass doors into a small vestibule and then through another set of smudged glass doors into the lobby.

Suddenly, a transformation took place ... it was as if I was thrust back in time. The small lobby was dimly lit and probably, with the exception of some changed light bulbs, was in its original circa 1931 state. The lobby floor was a dull brown and beige marble and was crying out for a deep cleaning and waxing. Hanging from the ceiling were four very small, ornate, bronze and crystal chandeliers that were probably last cleaned before they were put up prior to the hotel's grand opening. Off to the right was a tiny sitting area consisting of a frayed blue velvet love seat and a comfortable looking gold and blue club chair ... that is if the springs weren't broken. Adjacent to this chair was a wooden door that had a sign on it that read "Coffee Shop". Two elevators, a self-service one for guest use and a manually operated one used primarily by the bellmen, were positioned opposite the vestibule doors. An open-framed, prominent area on the left served as the reception desk with the permanent residents' and transient guests' mail and key cubicles visible in the background. Behind the reception desk and to the right was the barely visible plug switchboard;

to the left was the door to the executive office of the General Manager.

The tall, frail looking desk clerk standing behind the desk looked as if breathing was creating as difficult a chore for him as remaining erect. The poor chap looked as if he was going to expire before I could introduce myself.

I reached across the desk, extended my hand and gingerly said, "Good morning, I'm Herb Sokol."

The elderly clerk looked at me with a puzzled and confused expression and simply responded, "I am John Riley, the day-shift desk clerk."

I explained, that I was not a guest checking in but part of the new ownership group; I would be working with him and the rest of the hotel management team. He didn't seem to be expecting me and to say the least he was not very welcoming. Little did I realize that this was the beginning of a new, unimaginable and bizarre career in the hotel business ... an adventure that defies all reasoning and sensibility.

The Mission

It didn't take long for reality to start setting in. I firmly believe our investment group had not thoroughly examined the books of the previous owner ... at best it was a cursory glance. They moved forward with purchasing a thirty-five year lease purely on the basic principle that they could do better than the previous management group simply because they could. To accomplish this, the immediate goal was not to promote and increase business but to cut costs.

This was to be accomplished by me, the previous half-a doctor. I was expected to quickly learn all that could be learned, and to apply this knowledge by replacing the auditor, the incumbent General Manager, and perhaps even the day-shift desk clerk. The entire hotel staff, viewing me as an interloper and worse yet a company spy, made it rather difficult for me to gain insight into any job discipline immediately.

Strategic initiatives had to be taken quickly and the first was to get rid of the auditor and take his place. During my observation period, the auditor was either strutting about with an air of importance or was busy with his transcripts and data. I found it thoroughly amazing that it took me only three hours to replicate this individual's total weekly output.

The next step involved a lot of procrastination since I did not have the foggiest notion of a General Manager's job description. He played it close to the vest with no more than a hello and good-bye to offer in the way of intelligent discourse. Most of the time he was out of the hotel attending important association or business meetings at local taverns. Finally, after much pressure from the investment partners, I agreed to take his place as well. Surprisingly, nothing much changed. It was business as usual except that I was now made privy to every broken toilet, every theft, every employee gripe and every bad debt that was carried on the books.

With the original General Manager gone, I gained access to all thirty-one employees and soon befriended a few of them. Miss. Blackman, the day-shift switchboard operator was a very pleasant woman but very elderly, thin, and frail looking. She was truly a lovely lady but I recognized that given her age and condition her time was limited at the hotel. I didn't realize how limited until one tragic morning.

I was working at the desk in my executive office when I heard a loud thump! I raced out of the office to find that Miss. Blackman had fallen off her stool and had landed on the vinyl tile floor. I rushed to her side and found her struggling to breathe. While I picked her up, I shouted to the desk clerk (you know—the guy who was frail and looked like breathing was a chore) to call for an ambulance. I wondered ... could both of these workers have been here since the hotel opened? Anyhow, I carried Miss. Blackman to a second floor room and literally felt her pass away as I was placing her on the bed. I felt so helpless. I could neither ease her pain nor save her life. Tears flowed from my eyes; never had I experienced death so personally. Little did I know that this would be the first of many passings that would occur at The Roger Williams Hotel.

* * *

With every negative event, there is usually something good that presents itself as well. My mom had become a lost soul upon the death of my father a few months before. Aside from reading prurient novels, she had no interests whatsoever. I thought perhaps if I could persuade her to learn to work our antiquated, plug-switchboard she might become rejuvenated. As it turned out, she was most enthusiastic about the idea of working again. She learned and adapted quickly. Thus, Bella, the half-a-doctor's mother, became the day-shift telephone operator of a hotel and joined our illustrious staff.

At this time let me introduce some of our other key staff members:

<u>Miss. Flanagan - The Housekeeper:</u> Miss. Flanagan was very sweet and a devout Catholic. She stood 5' 6" tall and weighed over 200 pounds. She had extremely bowed legs and it seemed as if her sheer mass was crumbling the legs beneath her. This lady looked eighty-five, was probably only sixty, but moved and worked as if she was ninety-five. Most of her spare time, as well as much of the hotel's time, was spent in church. Miss. Flanagan was probably praying for the salvation of the hotel's poor, misfortunate guests.

<u>Tom - Day-Shift Desk Clerk:</u> Tom was very professional in his appearance as well as the presentation of himself and the hotel. He was always impeccably dressed in a neatly pressed suit, shirt and tie. He carried himself with an air of arrogance and was somewhat condescending toward both guests and fellow workers. He acted as if our rooms were precious gems that were too good for our average guest. Tom replaced the aged John Riley who had held this position on the day that I first arrived at the hotel.

<u>Ernie - The Engineer (a.k.a. Superintendent/Janitor):</u> Engineer is a loosely used title in hotel jargon. Ernie, a black man, was about 5' 7" tall. He had a pleasant face and an entirely bald dome with a fringe of neatly cropped brown hair. His almost baldhead sat atop a short neck that was attached to a solid, muscular frame. Actually, Ernie's body resembled a human tree trunk with arms like sturdy oak limbs. He possessed excellent communication skills considering that he was an uneducated man. Ernie demonstrated knowledge of plumbing and carpentry as well a capacity for compassion, sincerity, deviousness, treachery, thievery and entrepreneurship. This was definitely the person you would want walking in front of you, when you were confronted with potential bodily harm.

<u>Orson Mack - Handyman:</u> Orson was a quiet, unassuming, 6' tall, thin, black man who was an avowed enemy of Ernie's for reasons unknown to me. If any of the other employees knew the reason, they weren't willing to share it.

<u>Pepe - Carpet Layer/Plasterer/Tile-Man:</u> Pepe was an expatriate from Cuba and a true artist of his

craft. Although of small stature, his height was 5' 5" (even shorter than I was), and he was an extremely versatile and handy handyman. Pepe could create plaster walls that looked like marble and would easily lay carpet or Sonia depending upon his mood or state of sobriety. Unfortunately, when inebriated he became violent, menacing and threatening. He always carried a switchblade for protection. It was obvious, however, that he was not too adept in using it because a deeply carved X was etched on his forehead.

<u>Lincoln - Senior Bellman:</u> Lincoln was a gracious man. He took his job seriously and was particularly proud of his blue and gold uniform. One needed only to shake his hand and look in his eyes to know that this was a kind, considerate, friendly man. There were thirty-one employees in the hotel, and I'd say Lincoln was the one that my family and I grew to sincerely respect and care for the most. My son, David, especially liked *working* with him because Lincoln always shared his tips with him.

<u>Earl - Afternoon Bellman:</u> Earl was a dyed redheaded black who never spoke more than three consecutive words but he did his job well. He purchased my 1956 Buick convertible, one evening, when its transmission died in front of the hotel. I guess he or someone he knew had the ability to fix it.

<u>Joseph - Night Bellman:</u> Like Lincoln and Earl, Joseph was also black, but Joseph was educated and blessed with a lovely, velvety baritone voice. I believe he had aspirations to be a radio disk jockey but felt that racial prejudice during these times precluded him from this pursuit.

Joseph later became union shop steward, and it was rumored that he was also the local numbers runner for the *black mafia*. These leadership activities empowered him and he seemed to grow militant. He subsequently convinced the union that Lincoln's expensive and attractive uniform was demeaning to blacks and to coin his phrase, was a "monkey suit". Under the threat of a union walkout, and perhaps physical harm to myself, I promoted Joseph to desk clerk thus removing his "monkey suit" obligation. This was before affirmative action and, perhaps, the catalyst for it.

* * *

Talking about Joseph and his new position brings to mind the time when many televisions suddenly started disappearing from the hotel during the night-shifts. It was truly a mystery because the back doors were always locked at night. Thus, the televisions had to be taken out through the front lobby—past the desk clerk. I called the police but they were of no help. Since I could not think of any controls that I could use to help stop the thefts, I was prompted to assume my first role as hotel detective.

I sat in room 208 and overlooked the front entrance for two consecutive evenings and nights. It was during the second night of my stakeout that my affirmative action, rumored numbers runner clerk left his desk post, and the hotel, to transact some personal errands. Obviously, Joseph's lack of dedication to his promotion became apparent to some observant thief. While Joseph did his thing, the thief would do his; he entered through the front doors, quickly took a television and left again through the front doors.

Observing the thief from the safety and security and of my second story window, I bravely screamed, "Stop thief. I know who you are!"

When Joseph returned to the desk, I made him aware of my extra-curricular activities. I described to him in full detail, my sleepless nights and my observations. The lengths I went to, by sacrificing family time and sleep, in order to solve the mystery of the disappearing televisions seemed to impress Joseph. Especially, since he now knew that I was aware of the time he spent away from the desk. The thefts stopped with that incident.

* * *

It might seem to you while reading this that I am a racially prejudiced, bigoted individual. However, keep in mind my very isolated, Jewish ghetto upbringing. In the sixth grade I was shocked to find out that the new boy in my class, Charles Franks, was a Christian. Until that time I had never come face to face with a Gentile. My awareness of blacks came only from movie characters and television. My first encounter with real live black people was at the age of fourteen. I was in Coney Island with my cousins, Bernie Siegel and Marvin Goldstein, when we were introduced to four, young, enterprising blacks. These young businessmen convinced us to invest six nickels toward their college education fund with the relentless inducement of four waving knives.

With the above background in mind, please empathize and try to understand my dilemma. The hotel had thirty-one employees: nine were Caucasian, eight were Hispanic, and the balance were Black. In order to survive, I had to quickly adapt and develop sensitivity to and understanding of the diversified cultures within the hotel.

My daughter, Jodi, visited our home in Florida just at the time when I had finished writing the above segment.

After reading it, Jodi suggested, "Dad, readers are going to get the impression that you are a truly bigoted individual. Perhaps you should rewrite this."

"Jodi, though I try to color most of my experiences with a touch of humor, these feelings were what I had in 1960." Jodi tried her best to get me to rewrite. I finally responded, "I will think about it."

When I had a private moment, I looked up the definition of bigot. It was defined as "somebody who has very strong opinions, especially on matters of politics, religion, or ethnicity, and refuses to accept different views." Well, that clinched it for me. I sat down with Jodi and told her the following story about her brother, David.

One day, when David was about six years of age, he returned from playing outdoors and seemed very upset.

"What's wrong?" I asked, "Were you in a fight?"

"No, but I hate Aubrey. All my friends hate him."

"Did he say something mean to you or hit you?" I asked.

"No, I just hate him."

"David, you just don't hate someone; there has to be a reason for such feelings."

"I hate him because he's black. I hate all blacks."

I was momentarily speechless and then replied, "David that's not true. Do you hate Lincoln?"

"Of course not, he's not black" was his quick retort.

One can see that a child's innocence renders him color-blind, unless sadly, the influence of his friends pervade. They accept or reject a person simply by the individual's personality and behavior. I was extremely proud to inform Jodi, that by the end of my fifteen years at The Roger Williams Hotel, *I* had gained David's innocence.

Meeting Robert - Room 307

I arrived at the hotel at my normal time, 8:30 A.M., on a dreary April fool's morning in 1962. The rain just sat in the air almost like it couldn't decide if it wanted to fall or not, and it left me feeling like I couldn't decide if I wanted to work or not. But, of course, I didn't have the rain's luxury of choice—what I wouldn't have given to just sit there and do nothing. Anyhow, I was soon at my desk sipping the coffee that I had picked up at Chock Full O'Nuts.

I described the hotel lobby to you earlier ... my office was also circa 1931 décor. It certainly was not what a general manager would dream of for an executive suite. I worked in a dull, dingy, looking room; maybe it was 8' by 10', with just enough space for my mahogany desk, black metal filing cabinets and a few antiquated pieces of office equipment.

My desk, which I'm sure was splendid in its time, was now rutted and scratched to the point where the numerous piles of paperwork covering the desktop were an improvement. Perched on a table across the room on a one-inch piece of compressed old foam was my manual Underwood typewriter. This foam covering was obviously an attempt to salvage what was left of what was once a lovely veneer. A manual adding machine and check printer completed the office equipment. Clearly they represented two rare pieces ready for the National Museum of Office Relics.

What little light there was in the room came mostly from the fluorescent ceiling fixture that hummed loudly from the time I turned it on in the morning until I turned it off at the end of the workday. Just below the eight-foot ceiling was a small, single casement window, which opened onto the alley between the hotel and the neighboring Baptist Church. This I learned from the few times that I hoisted myself onto the filing cabinets, that lined the back wall, in an attempt to determine the source of strange thuds or squeals that I found too peculiar to ignore.

When I finally motivated myself to start the day, I stepped out of my office into the desk clerk's area where Tom, the day-shift desk clerk, was standing. He was facing out into the hotel lobby, through the window opening around the front desk, assisting a guest.

I waited for him to finish before walking by, since there was only a three-foot space behind him and I didn't want to disturb or distract him while he was attending to a guest. I always preferred that the desk clerks give as professional an appearance as possible, since the environment in which they worked clearly could not do it for them. As I waited, my eyes gazed up at the wall of 216 mailbox slots. I noticed that there were very few keys in the slots meaning that we were doing particularly well that week.

I stood there for a few minutes before actually noticing our guest. My heart started racing when I finally did. Sidney Poitier right here in my lobby? But no, this man was even more dashing and distinguished looking. I learned from Lincoln later that day, that this handsome, impeccably dressed, black guest was Mr. Robert Brown, a relatively new weekly tenant. Little did I know what this chance encounter would later lead to.

When our paths crossed in the lobby the following day, I introduced myself in the interest of developing better management/tenant relations, casually saying, "Good morning, Bob. I'm Herb Sokol, the General Manager of the hotel. It's a pleasure to meet you."

The look in his eyes was as if I had said, **Good morning, Mr. Hitler**. I was confused. What did I say? Should I run? Should I walk up to the gentleman waiting for the elevator behind him and pretend I had been addressing him? It was a difficult choice; I had no idea what I had said to offend this man.

After taking quick stock of the situation, I simply said, "Excuse me, Bob, but is something wrong? Is there something I can do to help you?"

"Yeah," he said gruffly, "Don't ever call me Bob! It's Robert or Mr. Brown. Never, and I mean never, call me Bob!"

I apologized and you can be sure I never made that mistake again. To this day, I still wonder what life had dealt this man under the name of Bob to cause such a hostile reaction. In any case, from that day on, he was Mr. Brown or Robert. And from that day on, that look of rage never crossed his face again ... well, at least not for the next few months.

Mr. Brown left the hotel early each morning and returned each day at 5:30 P.M. He always dressed in a Brooks Brothers style, carried a handsome attaché case, and portrayed the appearance of a successful executive.

The weeks passed and we developed a friendly banter. I was finally able to have a dialogue with a real business executive. We discussed what was happening in the city, politics, and the economy. I rarely got the chance to have this type of intellectual conversation with my other guests. I really enjoyed and looked forward to the opportunities when I could speak with Mr. Brown.

He began to advise me about investment opportunities that he was involved in; Robert referred to them as "cutting edge technology and global investments." His descriptions were always flowing with enthusiasm and excitement. I was frustrated that my finances, at the time, precluded me from contributing any venture capital to these investments.

Sometime around June, I noticed that Robert was starting to look a bit exhausted. He had deep, dark bags under his eyes, his posture was no longer perfectly erect, and most noticeably, he was beginning to look a little less tidy than usual.

THE MAFIA CAPER - ROOM 307

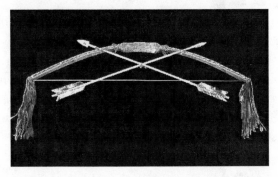

It couldn't have been more than two weeks later when Robert called down to the switchboard. In a loud, hysterical voice that none of us had ever heard from him before, he demanded that the switchboard operator tell me to come to room 307 immediately. (I'm amazed that I still remember the room numbers after all these years.) Of course, I responded immediately to his request. As I took the elevator up to the third floor, my mind was spinning with possible reasons for the hysterics. I approached his room hesitantly. Flashes of my first encounter with him were flooding my thoughts. Let's face it; I was concerned.

I knocked softly on the door—it opened instantaneously. Robert must have been waiting at the door for my arrival. His room, which had always been impeccably neat, was now in shambles and he appeared to be in total disarray. He was dressed in stained black pants that failed to stay up on his waist and a ripped white tee shirt that had yellowed beneath the armpits. I hardly recognized this man as the Mr. Robert Brown that I loved to talk with. His eyes looked as if they would pop from his head. To say the least—this was one angry man.

I stepped inside and Robert immediately began his tale. What he said didn't sound coherent ... what I could make out was that he had come home from work that day to find his room vandalized. After spending hours sifting through the rubble, he concluded that the Mafia had broken into his room and stolen certain undescribed, but desperately missed valuables. He swore that he would hold me liable for this breach of security, and with even more vengeance, he made it clear that he planned to get even with the *family members* responsible for this injustice.

I innocently suggested that he call the police and report the burglary. Maybe the police could help him achieve the revenge he so ardently sought. The face I saw before me suggested that my assistance was no longer appreciated. I left the room scratching my head, pondering what I had just witnessed, and speculating whether my friend, Mr. Brown, was dealing with a full deck. It also left me wondering how this young, naïve Jewish man from Brooklyn had managed to get himself into such a strange situation.

It was business as usual after that episode and I managed to put the incident behind me for most of my waking hours. I hadn't seen or heard from Mr. Brown in eight days and frankly I was hoping my luck would continue.

When I dared think about it, I feared that my rather insulated upbringing would not have prepared me for what might lie ahead. I worried about what my next encounter might be. Was it possible that a mobster had actually walked past me, or one of my employees, entered Mr. Brown's room and carried out his *valuables* without raising an eyebrow of suspicion? Thoughts such as this sent chills up my spine. The idea of such a presence in the hotel terrified me. Most nerve-racking was the thought that the mobster might return. If Mr. Brown's conclusion was wrong, what had really happened that day and what might come of it?

Well, my luck did not hold out.

Two days later, I was tending to some simple maintenance on the fourth floor when Flora, one of the maids, approached me and asked quietly in her sweet Hispanic accent, "Mr. Sokol, would you mind if I discussed a small problem with you about one of the rooms on the third floor?"

"Sure," I said, "I have a moment." In the back of my mind all I could think was, please, don't mention room 307, "What's the problem?" I fearfully inquired.

Flora opened her mouth and then closed it. She started again and then whispered, "Would it be okay if we spoke in there?" pointing to room 401, which she had just finished cleaning. "I'd rather not talk about this in the hallway. He may be around."

He? My fears were growing. What could he have done to her?

"Yes, of course, that would be fine," I answered as I entered the room and took a seat in the club chair in front of the window. She walked in behind me and quietly closed the door.

She paced for a minute or so and finally started to speak, "Last week ... I don't remember exactly ... oh yes, it was last Tuesday ... I remember now."

Whatever it was, it had taken her six days to tell me about it.

She continued, "Last week, I was to clean **room 307** and ...

An explosion went off in my head.

"I knock on door, as you tell us to do, and there was no answer. I knock again louder, just to make sure, and still no answer. Now, Mr. Sokol, you know I tell you truth always. I never want to walk in on nobody. So, when I hear no answer, I open door and turn to pull my cart in. When I get through door I turn around and ... well, what I see scare me clear to heaven. I scream. I know my knees are shakin' so much I can't move. I just stand there."

"Flora! **What? What did you see?**" I asked, truly petrified to hear the answer.

Was it a mob hit? Was the guy still there? Why hadn't I heard about this until now?

She waited a moment before continuing. "Mr. Sokol," she whispered, "I tell you this 'cause I'm scared. No maids will clean or go near there. We all scared."

She took a deep breath and continued, "I look up," she said as if visualizing it as she spoke, "and there, sittin'

46

in chair, where you sit now, was that man ... what's his name ... Mr. Brown. Look like he no change his clothes, no take shower in days, and he holdin' a bow and arrow! He was rantin' and ravin' somethin' about the dumb, 'scuse me please, 'fucks'. He say, they steal from him and he gonna shoot their brains out. He start to pull back arrow and something in me, thanks be to God, start workin' and I run out the door. Whether he shoot that thing I don' know. But he no look like he was playin'. You know I tell you truth always."

She took a moment to collect her thoughts, and then said desperately, "Please, Mr. Sokol, do somethin'. You talk sense to that man. And I hope you understan' I no clean room if he still there. I got family to take care of."

I was beginning to question my own sanity. Had she just told me that Robert Brown had threatened her with, of all things, a bow and arrow? Was he now playing Cowboys and Indians or something? Where the hell was I? No one had warned me that being a hotel manager would mean dealing with situations like this. What happened to the business executives, internationalists, and diplomats that I had looked forward to?

"Flora, please relax," I said trying as hard as I could to comfort her. I really did not want her to quit. She was a hard worker and ... I liked her. I also believed her.

"I understand that you are scared, and I don't blame you. Of course you shouldn't go into that room again," I said reassuringly.

I sat there thinking through the outrageous story I had just heard, and then asked, more to convince myself that I was still working with all my marbles than out of concern for Flora's honesty, "Did he really have a bow and arrow?"

"Yes, Mr. Sokol, a bow and arrow," she said, starting to calm down a bit. "I no see one before, except my boy's little toy, but that's what it is. And this one very big and no toy."

"Don't worry Flora. I'll take care of this and please let the other maids know that it is under control. Flora, thank you for telling me."

I left the room and went downstairs in a daze. I grabbed my coat, left the hotel and walked down East 31st Street to The Martinique Hotel; I remembered that there was a bar in the lobby. While practically stumbling onto a bar stool, I ordered myself a highball.

As I sipped my drink my fractured nerves began to settle down a little. I rarely ever had a drink before I started working at The Roger Williams Hotel. Every now and then when we got together with some friends I'd drink socially but I'd never been a drinker. After hearing this story, though, I simply needed a drink. I'd heard people on television and in the movies say they needed a drink but I had no idea what they really meant—until now. Yeah, I'd told Flora I'd handle it. But what was I supposed to do? I'd never been in a situation like this before and I was probably as scared as Flora, if not more.

Why did I take on this responsibility in the first place? Sure, manage a hotel. From the outset it seemed like a glamorous desk job; I'd oversee the bellmen, maids and other employees. I would make sure the books were kept properly and that the hotel looked as presentable as possible, given what I had to work with. No one ever told me I'd be handling mob break-ins and guests waving bows and arrows! What had I signed up for here?

I was suddenly dreaming of the dull days behind the counter working in a pharmacy as half-a-doctor and dealing with the *yentas*. Perhaps I had made a mistake. As the alcohol warmed its way through my body, I began to face the facts. The situation was handed to me and somehow I would have to deal with it. I had to confront Robert; at least I thought I should.

As I sat on the bus, on the way home that night, I kept going over Flora's account in my head. Maybe I should call the police and let them handle it. After all, a bow and arrow—I couldn't risk letting any of my employees get hurt. But I liked Robert; I sincerely liked the man, at least the Robert who originally checked in. These last few occurrences were totally out of character for him. Maybe he had problems at work or in his family (if he had one). Maybe he had just lost control. He hadn't actually hurt anyone—yet.

After a nice relaxing dinner with Annette and the children, I was starting to put things into perspective. Later when the kids were asleep and Annette and I finally had some time alone, hopefully, she could help me sort through this mess. She was always so logical. If there was anything I needed desperately right now it was pure logic.

"Annette," I said as we settled onto our comfy living room couch, "Do you remember that weird incident I told you about last week, when Robert Brown insisted that the Mafia had broken into his room?"

"Yes, of course, I remember. Don't tell me they came back?" she asked mockingly.

"No. But it's gotten a whole lot stranger. Today one of the maids, Flora, approached me in the hallway. She was very upset and needed to talk. When she went to clean Robert's room last week ... " I began, and then proceeded to tell her the entire story exactly as Flora had told it to me.

When I finished, she stared at me with a curious look in her eyes and said, "A bow and arrow? You can't be serious!"

"I'm afraid I am," and somehow this time I started to smile. I was suddenly seeing the humor in the situation. We laughed for a bit until I remembered that I still had to handle this ridiculous, and possible dangerous, situation. "So, any ideas?"

"Well, you do have to do something, but I don't know what. From things you have told me in the past I always thought of Robert as such a sweet, respectable guy."

"I know. That's the problem."

"Maybe you should try talking to him. If it gets you nowhere, you can always call the police ... but perhaps there really is some rational explanation for this. It is kind of hard to imagine one, but maybe. Do you think he's been rehearsing for a play or something?"

"It sure would make a good play but, no, I don't think so. However, I do think you're right about talking to him. What's the worst that could happen?"

"He could shoot you with that crazy bow and arrow! If you're going to talk to him, **please be careful**! If he starts doing anything crazy, just get out of there and call the police. Don't be a hero. You really weren't cut out for that role."

She was right. "Okay. I'll figure out some way to approach him about all of this tomorrow and I promise, I'll be careful. I may be the manager of that place, but I'm not crazy ... at least not yet."

On the ride into work the next day, I decided I would simply approach him directly with my concerns and ask him for an explanation. When I got to the hotel, I decided to go straight up to his room before I could chicken out. Feeling a surge of bravery, I knocked on the door. It opened. Robert looked even more disheveled than he did the week before.

"Robert, can we talk for a minute? Something's come up that I need to discuss with you," I said without accusation.

"Sure. Come on in." He spoke with the same casual, friendly tone of voice that I remembered from the past. "What's up?"

I stepped inside and looked nervously around. There, resting prominently on his bed was the bow and arrow. "**It's about that**," I said pointing to the weapon.

"What? The bow and arrow?" he asked almost innocently.

"Yeah. The bow and arrow." His nonchalant tone was starting to irritate me. "Why is it here and what do you plan on doing with it?"

"You're kidding, right? You can't tell me you forgot about the break-in. I'm just trying to defend myself."

"Defend yourself all you want, but when you start threatening my employees ..."

"Hold it a minute! So that's what this is all about. I didn't threaten anybody. Flora knocked on the door and then just walked in. I didn't let her in or anything. I thought it was them."

"But when she was in your room, you certainly must have realized it wasn't the Mafia."

"Look, I'm not planning to hurt anyone who's not looking to hurt me. It was an honest mistake. When I realized it I apologized, but she was already out the door."

It couldn't be that simple, could it? Was he so blind with rage that he honestly didn't realize it was Flora until she was gone? He could have seriously hurt her!

"Listen, Robert, why a bow and arrow?" I asked, curious to hear his answer.

"Well, a few years ago, the police got this bug about me. They picked me up and threw me into jail. They convicted me on false charges. I didn't do anything. You know me better than that, but now I have this criminal record."

"You have a criminal record? Yeah, I'm sure it must have been a mistake," I said trying to keep on his good side, not knowing what to believe at this point.

"Anyway, I'm not looking to go back to jail, so I got this bow and arrow. They can't arrest me for carrying a bow and arrow, at least not as far as I know. The last thing I want is for the police to decide to come looking for me again and find me with a gun or something."

"Yeah. A gun wouldn't be a good idea, but do you really feel you need a weapon?" I inquired.

"You kiddin'? Those guys come back here? They come showin' their faces round here one more time, I'm gonna skewer the bastards! I'm gonna skewer those suckers that ripped me off!"

That all too familiar rage had returned. Once again I tried to convince him that the police could do a better job of defending him than he could, but he was convinced that the police were out to get him too. I'd gotten my answer, now I just had to decide what to do with it.

Before I left I tried, as tactfully as I could, to warn Robert that I couldn't have him threatening my employees with weapons of any sort. I respected his need to get even with the people that stole from him but first, he'd better be sure he had the right people and second, he'd better be extra sure to do whatever he planned outside the hotel premises. Otherwise, I would be forced to put our relationship aside and call the police.

I left almost as confused as when I had entered. Could he possibly be telling me the truth? Clearly, he had a criminal record. Having seen his recent behavior, I was finding it hard to believe that the charges had been false.

If I were to call the police, what would I tell them? A tenant had threatened a maid with a bow and arrow? Would they believe me? He hadn't actually shot the thing. If they questioned him, he'd tell them he thought she was threatening him. He was just defending himself— but look at her and look at him! How could they possibly believe he felt threatened? Sure he had a right to defend himself but didn't he have to act reasonably? Robert's actions didn't strike me as being quite reasonable.

I wanted to do the right thing but I certainly didn't want to turn Robert into the police and end up getting on his bad side, especially if it wasn't going to help this strange state of affairs. From past experiences I figured that the police would just ignore the whole situation, let him go, and I would be left in a very undesirable position. Again, he hadn't hurt anyone. Maybe Flora really did leave too fast and therefore, didn't have a chance to hear his apology.

THE NAKED COUPLE
IN THE ALLEY

The next morning, as I approached the hotel entrance on my way to work, something unusual caught my eye. As I passed the alley between the church and the hotel (you know—the place where I was first mugged) I noticed Robert loitering in the alleyway. I tried not to dwell on it but I did notice that he was still there in the evening. The next morning he was there again and he hadn't left by the time I went home again that evening. He looked like a vagrant ... unshaven and completely unkempt. His eyes were darting back and forth with a wild look; his body was jerking right and left, and forward and back like a wild boar defending itself against a predator. My curiosity and concern were getting the better of me. Finally, I gathered up enough chutzpa to approach him and ask what he was doing in the alley.

With eyes blazing, he shrieked at me, "You've done nothing to apprehend those Mafia culprits! I'm staking out the place. I'll catch those bastards when they come back!"

It was obvious to me that it was time to get out of there while I still could, so I turned and quickly departed. I really didn't want to get any more involved than I already was. Thankfully, he was no longer in the hotel! Somehow, over the next two days, I managed to forget about Robert.

On Friday afternoon, I was sitting at my desk in deep deliberation over what I wanted for lunch. Should I have corned beef or pastrami? Cole slaw or potato salad? Suddenly, coming from what seemed like the alley, I heard a piercing scream followed by loud sobs and pleas for help. I called the police immediately. Then without thinking, I foolishly ran out to see what was going on. Following the sounds of the cries that continued to penetrate the unusually cool June air, I raced toward and then into the alley

What I found was beyond my wildest imagination! There was Robert standing with his feet in a wide stance, knees bent, his back hunched over just enough to add an intensely insane quality to the image before me. He was again jumping left to right and back left again but now he was wildly brandishing the largest butcher knife I'd ever seen. Beyond Robert, in the far right corner, I saw a young man and woman flat out naked. The couple was huddled together on the cold concrete and shivering more from fear than from the temperature of the air. Their clothes were strewn in a random heap not far from them.

Given my encounters over the past few weeks, my first response was oddly enough to laugh, but I tried hard to control myself. My urge to laugh quickly changed when I saw Robert's eyes popping out of his head again. **It was really a scary sight**! I gathered myself together and tried to assert myself.

"Robert, what the fuck are you doing?"

"I got them! I got the Mafia creeps that ripped me off! I told you I'd get them," he yelled almost gleefully.

"Robert, why are they naked?" I asked, attempting to maintain my calm and get to the bottom of this while retaining my appearance as his ally.

"Isn't it obvious? I had them undress so they wouldn't escape," he answered most emphatically ... as if I was the stupid one here.

I was at a loss. I had no idea what to say or do next. Thankfully, I heard sirens approaching.

You've just got to picture the scene the two cops saw as they raced into the alley with their guns drawn: first there was me, dressed in a business suit, bewildered and frantic; past me there was Robert, wielding his giant sized butcher knife, and doing his wild boar maneuvers; and finally at the end of the alley, a young couple, totally stripped, cowering, and petrified.

To add to this scene, in case I wasn't distressed enough, the younger of the two cops appeared extremely nervous. I couldn't help but think that he was probably on his first *serious* call. As he came running down the alley, his hands kept trembling. Suddenly—his revolver popped open and, I kid you not, his bullets started falling out. Click, click, click, one by one they dropped to the ground. I've got to tell you, New York's finest frightened me more than Robert with any weapon!

Just in case I hadn't had enough excitement for the day, the police, unable to immediately sort out the situation, thought it best to drag all of us down to the precinct. So Mr. Robert Brown; my two, now clothed, new friends; and I took a scenic ride in a paddy wagon and were then ushered into the police station.

After lengthy questioning, it was discovered that the young couple had been on a lunch break and harmlessly walked into the alley to smoke a joint. Although emotionally traumatized, they were physically unharmed. (However, they may never smoke a weed again.) The police upon discovering Robert's prior criminal record, which was much more lengthy than Robert had let on, finally acknowledged that I was a hero and not a perpetrator. They finally gave me permission to go back to work. Now, what was it that I decided to have for lunch? Was that pastrami or corned beef? Did I even have an appetite?

Robert ended up in jail and I had a great deal of trouble accepting the fact that he was a *real, live criminal.* Even after everything I'd been through with him, and all that I witnessed, it was still hard to shake the memories of our friendship. I even visited him in jail once. Somehow I felt sorry for him. I believed this nice, educated man must have been a victim of sorts.

To this day, I don't know if anyone really broke into his room or if it was all a figment of his imagination. All I can say is that I had now been inducted into the world of the bizarre, or more accurately, into the life of the General Manager of The Roger Williams Hotel.

THE SEDUCTION -
ROOM 910

We were predominately an extended stay hotel because all of our rooms had a private bath, small kitchenette with two-burner gas stove, sink, and lowboy refrigerator. Nevertheless, we also rented rooms on a daily, weekly, monthly, and on quite a few occasions, an hourly basis. In addition, we had forty-five very demanding rent-controlled tenants who paid anywhere from $60 to $85 per month and had the privilege of enjoying a Madison Avenue, midtown, residential address.

To gain insight into my responses to certain incidents that took place at The Roger Williams Hotel, it might help if you knew a bit more of my heritage and background. My paternal grandfather was a European rabbi of some renown. Family members have informed me that he was published and was looked upon as the Mayor of his "shtetl" (town) back in Poland. He was rigid, absolutely unbending in his beliefs, and spent his days studying the Talmud.

His son, my father, feigned his religious beliefs for his father's sake. Both men, however, lived their days following the guidelines of fidelity and family. My upbringing was not one of religious observances but one of high morals, charity, and good work ethics. With this in mind, try to imagine me working in this hotel.

Upon entering thru its portals, I felt like the male version of Alice in Wonderland. The hotel's internal guest activity resembled absolutely nothing that I had previously experienced or could have even imagined. Positioned in the center of a major metropolis, this was my land of temptations and illusions. Many beautiful women checked in. Seductions abounded. Occasionally, high-class call girls set up their entrepreneurial ventures here. At other times pimps managed to get by our lax security and book rooms for their stable. A wise man once gave me counsel (not that I required it), "Herb, never shit where you eat." I was content to just be a voyeur.

* * *

One of our regular monthly guests was Mrs. Kane in room 910. She was a southern belle who had a distinctively, heavy drawl; was approximately forty-seven years of age; attractive; had long, wavy brown hair; sparkling blue eyes; a good figure; and an outgoing, gregarious personality. I assumed she was a businesswoman, but in truth, I really had no idea what her activities were during the day.

Because of her vivacious personality, one definitely would not think of her as the kind of person that would be lonely. She never walked by the front desk without an acknowledgement or a friendly good morning or good evening. After awhile, her hellos became longer and her good evenings started to linger. Our relationship started progressing from political discussions to personal thoughts and feelings. Her good mornings became more and more animated and on occasion, at chance meetings in the lobby, she would brush up against me. She started to act coquettish and I started to feel uncomfortable. Was she flirting with me?

Abruptly, her schedule and personality changed. Mrs. Kane stopped going out each morning and remained in her room. She responded in a bitterly tone to the maids and bellmen and complained about dripping faucets and a broken television. I was left countless messages to come to her room to see its deplorable condition as well as to hear about the inferior service she was receiving. I would respond to each request with a work-order or a follow-up for the housekeeper.

One hot, humid Sunday in August, our guest buzzed the switchboard and asked to be connected to me. When I answered the phone she started grumbling that her air conditioner had broken down. Since the engineer, Ernie, was off on Sundays I told her I would send a handyman up to check it out.

She started to shriek at the top of her lungs so that I could have heard her without the phone, "Your staff is comprised of incompetents. Ernie has checked the unit numerous times and has resolved nothing."

Mrs. Kane insisted that I come up, see for myself, and immediately order a new unit for her room. Sundays were generally quiet days at the hotel and I looked forward to them because it gave me an opportunity to read the *New York Times*, relax, and goof off a little. Unfortunately, the newspaper would have to wait. I grabbed the service elevator and went up, not only with reluctance, but also with resentment because our guest was disrupting my routine. In addition, I felt very agitated because she had been screaming at me.

I knocked at the door and identified myself. The door opened, I stormed in, and walked directly to the defective window air-conditioning unit. My mind was so set on checking out the air conditioner that I barely heard the clicking sounds coming from behind me. Reaching the window I placed my hand in front of a forceful flow of frigid air emanating from the unit.

Exclaiming, "God Damn!" I turned around and bumped into her.

She had positioned herself directly behind me. It took only a second to realize she was clad only in a bright pink terrycloth robe. With what seemed like one effortless motion, the robe suddenly slipped to the floor and both her arms embraced me about the neck. Here I was nose-to-nose, and breast-to-breast with a naked woman who was not my wife! This was a total dilemma. I stood there caught off-guard, embarrassed, and stammering for words.

The only thing I could think to say was, "I'm late for a meeting. I have to go."

I threw her arms off me and dashed hell-bent for the door. She had engaged the safety chain as well as the double lock. I fiddled frantically with them and she stood naked behind me—frantically pulling at my jacket. She desperately enticed and begged me to stay.

I can honestly state that I was not late for my meeting. I could just hear the remarks of my Brooklyn friends (who were all unmarried at the time) when they heard about this situation.

"Ya mean ya didn't screw her?"

"You did what? You left her standing there naked?"

"Are you crazy man?"

What they probably could not understand is that many of my guests were extremely lonely and depressed. Some were delusional and belonged in an appropriate institution. Even if I was not married and had not taken vows of fidelity, I could not imagine exploiting these unfortunate souls. Our relationship diminished after that service call and Mrs. Kane never complained to me about another air-conditioning problem.

As I sit here, jotting down these amusing events, I cannot restrain myself from chuckling out loud. Looking back to the 1960's, I realize I was in my late twenties and early thirties and responsible for running a midtown Manhattan hotel. My business card read, "General Manger" ... the reality of it all was that the card should have read, "Keeper of the Asylum". Looking back, I now wonder if I did not become a patient in this asylum also. I certainly did participate in bizarre events that, to this day, my family and friends still regard with total disbelief.

THE PIMP ENCOUNTER - ROOM 617

Previously, I stated the feelings and sensations I experienced as I looked upon the edifice of The Roger Williams Hotel on my first day. I mentioned that I was filled with a surge of excitement and anticipation as I imagined myself greeting dignitaries, business executives and perhaps on occasion, super models and actors from the Broadway Theater. Unfortunately this was not to be. My true excitement came from devastating pipe breaks, fixing toilets, and evicting dead-beat transients. The only time we saw real business people was on days when the city was packed and oversold (and that didn't happen too often).

Though the hotel was referred to as a midtown hotel, it was actually on East 31st Street and Madison Avenue which was too far south to be in the true hectic midtown area and too far east to be part of Broadway activity. The Madison Avenue Baptist Church, the owner of the property, occupied the first four stories on the Madison Avenue side, and their presence precluded liquor from being sold on the hotel premises. Because of this, the previous General Manager had to meet and drink with management employees from hotels such as the Roosevelt and the Commodore off our premises. He coddled them so that they would refer their overflow guests to our hotel when the town was filled. Of course, they would receive the usual commensurate commissions for their efforts. They referred guests somewhat reluctantly for we were perceived to be well below their standards.

In the beginning, I refused to accept this perception of my hotel and spent time and funds knocking on doors, advertising, and even established *key clubs* to entice those frugal individuals that required hourly rates. Though some progress was made, I realized it would be best to keep what we had and slowly build on our base of rent controllers, weeklies, asylum dwellers and the occasional quickies or jumpers as some called them. We were vigilant in our attempts to exclude pimps, but not always successful. Though some pimps had excellent payment records, most offered only trouble and a negative reputation for the hotel.

In the event that any of our guests did not make their payment on time—be it daily, weekly, or monthly, I would plug their room. In essence this entailed placing half a key into the lock, which jammed it and prevented the delinquent guest from using their key to enter their room.

On one occasion, I had to plug the room of a pimp who apparently had entered into a recessionary period in his practice. Two days after this I went to his room with a bellman, quickly packed his meager belongings and placed them in our storage area. Given their virtually insignificant value, I suspected we would never see this *entrepreneur* again. Mistake!

On the fourth day after the lock out, he presented himself and loudly demanded his belongings. I calmly presented his debt to him. After some "mother fuckers" and some other unflattering, choice adjectives, he paid the bill. I then instructed the bellman to get the pimp's belongings. He returned momentarily with the packed bag and handed it to the man. Good riddance, I thought.

Second mistake! The next day he reappeared and asked for me. Scowling and with menacing actions, he demanded the return of his earrings.

I politely responded, "Mr. Gates, I personally oversaw the gathering of your personal effects and their placement inside your suitcase."

Bigger mistake! His language became more abusive and menacing, as if that was even possible, and I began to fear for my safety. Fortunately, Bella was at the switchboard and could hear everything that was going on. My very frightened mother had already summoned the police. Upon their welcomed arrival, they witnessed a raving, incoherent, nut job, and promptly carted Roosevelt Gates off to Bellevue Psychiatric Hospital.

Guess who reappeared three days later? You're right, Mr. Roosevelt Gates. He was unshaven, filthy, and perhaps a little crazier than he was a few days ago. Without hesitation, I called for help. The men in blue were the same cops that had responded the last time. One of them took me aside and presented me with an irresistible offer. For $50 they would rough him up. For $200 I would never have to see him again. I made the appropriate investment and never had to deal with Mr. Gates again.

THE FRIDAY PARTNER

It was late afternoon on a Friday in November 1961, when a gypsy cab pulled up to the entrance of the hotel. A man in his twenties dressed in dirty jeans and a shabby plaid flannel shirt emerged from the vehicle and proceeded to enter the hotel. His only luggage was a brown paper bag that he carried in his left hand. Mr. Brooks, a resident, had just exited the self-service elevator and nodded to the young gentleman that I hoped would be our new guest. Except for these two people and myself, the lobby was empty.

Our, hopefully, new guest approached me and with his right hand now inside the paper bag, loudly proclaimed, "This is a stick up—give me all your money and nobody will get hurt!"

I may not be a genius, but I am smart enough to know that when a possible gun is pointed at you, the best thing to do is cooperate. So I gave him the money—after all, it wasn't really mine anyway. I quickly scooped whatever bills were in our cash drawer, handed them to the man and watched as he calmly walked out and got back into the waiting cab. I called the police and after a brief report it was business as usual.

In the late afternoon, the following Friday, the same cab pulled up alongside our marquee. Our holdup man got out and again entered through our glass doors. You would think that after last Friday he could have afforded a new wardrobe or at least a cleaner's bill. But no, he was still wearing the same clothing as before ... they were just a little dirtier. He did, however, carry a new brown paper bag. Once again he requested my hard earned proceeds and again I handed it over without hesitation. He quickly departed.

When the police came this time, I asked if they could possibly stake out our place in hopes of catching the robber in the act. They said they would take it under consideration. The third Friday our partner showed up again and once more I gave him his weekly share of the profits. The police were of no help and I felt utterly at a loss as to how to deal with this problem. Maybe we should just accept it as a reality and automatically cut our new colleague a share.

But I was angry and frustrated now and I decided to take more aggressive action. I put a large monkey wrench under the counter with the hope that if this man could be distracted, I could smack the bag/weapon out of his hand. All week long I paced back and forth in my small office ... planning and anticipating my reactions to our unwanted partner. The fourth Friday came and went uneventfully. The following week was even worse for me. My nerves were completely on edge. I started to believe I wouldn't be able to follow through with my plan. After three weeks, I recognized that he must have liquidated his shares in The Roger Williams Hotel. Fortunately, for all concerned, he must have made other investments for we never saw him again.

THE .45 CALIBER

The hotel was very vulnerable to hold-ups. Fortunately for me, most occurred after midnight. Unfortunately, for my night clerk, these incidents brought him a few nights of terror and one nasty bump on his head. However, two such incidents occurred during the daytime and I remember them well. One was the previously mentioned "Friday Partner" and the second was the ".45 Caliber".

Tom, our day-shift desk clerk, was in his sixties and due to retire at the end of the month. One afternoon, at the beginning of February, I was in my office when I became aware of a lively exchange of words coming from the desk area. The volume kept increasing and it was starting to sound heated. I suddenly realized that a holdup man was demanding money and the desk clerk was refusing to give it to him. Tom had only a few weeks left before retirement and was refusing to hand over money that wasn't even his. What's with this man, I thought, **is he crazy?**

I quickly approached the desk at the same time that the robber leapt over the counter, brandished a gun and shouted at me, "Get this fuckin' lunatic away from me."

He clubbed Tom on the head and shoved him onto the floor of my office.

I then felt his weapon against my forehead and heard him scream, "**Gimme the fuckin' money.**"

It is interesting to note how people react under stressful situations.

Though the cold steel was pressing against my temple ... I spoke calmly, "Sir, the cash is in a drawer under this slanted work desk, so with your permission I will open it."

He stared at me with protruding eyes and then loudly answered, "Open the fuckin' drawer."

I opened the drawer and continued, "Sir, with your permission, I will take out the bills."

I removed the bills, placed them on the desk, and then replied, "Sir, under this drawer are additional bills, with your permission, I will take them out also."

This time he said nothing but pressed the gun more firmly to my head. With this encouragement, I removed and placed the additional funds on the desk. The man looked crazed and I thought for sure he was going to shoot me.

Instead, he shoved me through my office doorway and yelled, "Join your mother fuckin' friend!"

In an instant the robber jumped back over the counter and was gone. Calmly, I picked myself up off the floor and checked on Tom's status. He was trembling but thankfully not hurt badly. Hopefully, he realized the stupidity of his actions. Once again *our friendly blue* were called—they took just a few minutes to arrive. The cops wanted to know exactly what happened and then asked me if I could describe the perp.

"He looked like a giant .45 automatic," I responded.

I was told that I then proceeded to lose all color and drop to the floor. I was out cold.

HE PUNCHED ME - ROOM 710

After the Great Depression my Mom, Dad, and I lived with my paternal grandmother, grandfather—who was a Rabbi, and my two aunts and their respective families in a house that the congregation of Ulster Heights, (the mountainous suburb of Ellenville, New York) made available to their Rabbi/Shochet. It was close quarters but everyone was happy to be together and have a roof over their heads ... I don't think anyone complained.

Sometimes my parents took advantage of various landlords' generosity when they offered three to six months free rent as an inducement to fill their vacant apartmentbuildings. We went from free rent to family ... to free rent ... and back to sharing with family again.

In August 1941, Mom, Dad, my sister Carol and I moved to a third floor, three room, walk-up apartment in Brooklyn. You can imagine my mother's excitement as we entered this apartment. It was her first true home. Not wanting me underfoot, as she carefully unpacked our meager belongings, she firmly suggested I walk down to the lobby and play. In those years, parents did not have fear of strangers attacking or kidnapping their children. It was almost instinct to send kids down to play by themselves.

As a seven-year old I was rather shy but not fearful. So I obediently ran down the three flights and hung out in the front lobby by myself. After about fifteen minutes, I was entirely bored and started to hop on my left foot and then the right foot. Before I could switch again to my left foot ... a redheaded, grossly freckled fat kid rudely interrupted me.

"Hey, what's your name," he shouted.

"My name is Herby," I timidly answered.

" I am Jackie. What kind of fan are you?" was his next inquiry.

I stood there dumbstruck. I knew of only two fans ... an electric one and a paper hand fan that my Mom occasionally used. I guess the fat kid interpreted my silence as defiance or a fear of divulging some horrible secret. He took exception to my non-response and immediately started to pummel me with both of his fat fists.

With each strike he yelled, **"You're a Yankee fan— you're a Yankee fan!"**

I would even admit to being an electric fan if he would only stop hitting me. Finally, I got his message and screamed, "I am a Yankee fan, I am a Yankee fan."

Hearing my proclamation, Jackie stopped punching me and left feeling smug and satisfied. From that day on Brighton Beach had at least two Yankee fans.

Growing up, I always managed to avoid physical confrontations. I could talk my way out of most difficulties and if that didn't work, my fleetness would hold me in good stead. Aside from Jackie, and my dad smacking me once for saying the *shmuck* word, no one else had ever struck me until now ... .

* * *

Steven Katz was a monthly, permanent guest. A man in his thirties, Steve lived a lonely existence. He was gruff, mean, anti-social, and as if that wasn't enough, he had a very unnerving habit. He would stand with his feet apart, planted firmly on the ground, and stare at people. I got the impression that he had no visitors and got no phone calls. His only communication with the world seemed to come from countless magazine subscriptions. His chosen vocation as a cab driver was appropriate for it required limited verbal interaction and effort on his part.

Personally, I chose to avoid him whenever possible and cringed at the thought of having to share even an elevator ride with him. I think that the desk clerks felt the same way because I noticed that they would place his mail on the counter rather than hand it to him directly. This enabled them to turn away quickly and avoid his penetrating eyes. One morning, while I was covering for the day clerk during his coffee break, Mr. Katz exited the elevator and headed straight toward the desk. Turning quickly, I feigned performing some chore. I could feel his piercing eyes on my back as I continued with my improvised task.

He cleared his throat with a loud, "Ahem!"

Realizing I was acting childishly, I slowly turned to place his mail on the counter. Instead of reaching for the mail, he grabbed my jacket and pulled me toward him. He followed this maneuver with a smashing fist to my head and fled out the door. I was knocked to the ground more enraged than hurt.

After Mr. Katz punched me, rage took over common sense. I grabbed the large monkey wrench, previously set aside for our "Friday Partner" and took flight after our guest with the staring eyes. Through the large picture windows of our coffee shop the patrons having breakfast were able to observe a lunatic running down East 31st Street, thrashing a monkey wrench at some imaginary foe. Mr. Katz was nowhere to be found. I turned onto Madison Avenue and continued running until I reached East 32nd Street. Taking hold of a trashcan on the corner, I stopped and tried to catch my breath. Beating the air with the wrench must have relieved and diminished my anger ... I was now able to think more clearly. After a few more moments I headed back to the hotel and called the police. Though I knew that my immature attitude precipitated the encounter at the desk, I still had him arrested for assault. The charges were ultimately dropped and Mr. Katz continued staring at people and I continued avoiding him.

MR. BIERMAN'S LOVER - ROOM 1118

M r. Alan Bierman was a monthly tenant in room 1118. I believe he was Vice President of Finance for a publicly traded company that manufactured adding machines and other office products. He was the kind of guest any hotel manager would love to have; he gave me no grief, no complaints and no trouble of any nature. Though I didn't know him well, he presented himself as a true gentleman, mild mannered, always neatly attired in a business suit, and friendly in a shy, inhibited way. Mr. Bierman was in his late fifties, had a wiry build, wore round wire-rimmed glasses, and had a shock of white hair. I assumed he was a bachelor since I had never seen him with a lady friend or any friend for that matter.

One day, the *New York Daily News* headlined a story about a brutal slaying that occurred a few blocks from the hotel. They described in gruesome detail the savage beating of the victim but offered no other information except for the fact that the victim had been attacked not long after leaving a local pub.

Three days later I was covering for the evening desk clerk who had called in sick. It was around 8 P.M. when detectives from the 21ˢᵗ precinct paid me a visit. They explained that they were investigating a brutal slaying and hypothesized that the killer preyed on homosexuals.

"But, how can I help? I have no idea who he is. Why are you here?" I asked as my stomach started turning.

"Mr. Sokol, you have a homosexual guest in your hotel whom we believe is the killer's lover," answered one of the cops.

"Are you kidding me?" I questioned.

I knew we had plenty of crazies in the hotel, and it wasn't as if we didn't have gays as guests, but I found it hard to accept the fact that any of my guests could be involved with a murderer.

"And who might this guest be?" I inquired.

"I believe you have a man by the name of Alan Bierman residing here and we suspect that he might be harboring the killer."

I was absolutely stunned when I heard this name; I could hardly think or speak.

After taking a few deep breaths and trying to regain my composure, I asked, "What can I do to help?"

One of the cops said, "We would like you to take us up to his room."

His partner, added, "Don't worry you won't be in any danger."

I called Earl away from his bell stand and asked him to cover the desk for me. I took a key to room 1118 and led the two detectives into the manual service car. We proceeded to the eleventh floor and since Mr. Bierman's room was directly adjacent to the elevator shaft, we did not have to walk far.

I pointed to the room, offered the key to the officer, and started to return to the elevator. One cop placed his finger to his lips, motioning silence, and whispered to me, "Just knock on the door."

At the time I couldn't understand why two big strapping police officers couldn't do their own knocking, but that was quickly clarified. While I knocked, the two cops drew their revolvers, jumped aside, and left me exposed to the possibility of deadly gunfire.

I couldn't believe they did this to me! I swiftly ducked out of the way and whispered loudly, **"Damn it, I'm getting the hell out of here."** I grabbed the elevator and left the cops to battle the alleged murderer and his lover by themselves.

It turned out that neither the suspected murderer nor Mr. Bierman were in the room at the time. Our guest was ultimately apprehended approximately ten days later. He was vindicated and wisely chose a new dating service.

THE LADY IN THE SHROUD - ROOM 1001

It was 9:30 PM on a cold, depressing Halloween night. Earlier, I had phoned Annette to let her know that the clerk that worked 4 P.M. to 12 A.M. shift had called in sick **again**. Since the day clerk refused to pull a double, I would have to cover the shift. As I was about to pick up a magazine, the front doors opened. A woman entered so quickly it appeared as if a gust of wind had blown her in front of me. She asked if she could be accommodated with a single room for this evening. I nodded in the affirmative even though I had a sick feeling, because of her appearance, that I was making a mistake. Let me explain: her hair was in disarray and her eyes looked glazed; she seemed to be staring off into space. Her once stylish print dress was torn on one side, part of her hem was hanging down, and her brown pumps were covered with mud. Do you think that was enough of a hint? I guess not for me.

She signed the register as Mrs. Karen Wright, Havana Cuba. Her hands shook with tremors as she counted out the payment for one night's stay. I wondered—could she be a boat person that had missed Miami and drifted north, ending up at East 31st Street and the East River.

True, this was not an upscale hostelry but I hoped we had not descended to this woman's apparent level. However, her money was real and her stay was going to be brief. I gave Joseph, the bellman, the key to 1001. He picked up her bag and escorted her to the small corner room facing the rear.

At 11:30 P.M. I received a frantic call from a guest on the tenth floor. The caller was worried because she heard what she described as *blood-curdling screams* emanating from a room nearby. Joseph had left the hotel on an errand for another guest. Therefore, I had to leave the desk unattended as I quickly took the service elevator to the tenth floor. As I exited the elevator I immediately heard the screams. They were coming from the corner room that I had rented to Mrs. Wright earlier in the evening. As I approached room 1001, the screaming suddenly stopped. Instead, I now heard the sound of glass fragments crunching beneath my shoes. The light bulb that once illuminated the corner area of the hallway had been smashed and I was in eerie and total darkness.

Ominous thoughts started to explode in my head. Had Mrs. Wright been assaulted? Was she murdered? Was the killer still there? My eyes had not yet adjusted to the darkness when the door began to very, very slowly open. I could make out a human figure standing there.

In a few seconds I was able to see more clearly. Framed in the doorway was Mrs. Wright in what appeared to be a white shroud. Her hair looked even more disheveled than earlier in the evening. She gave out another one of her shrill, bloodcurdling scream and raised her hand. I could now clearly see an extremely long butcher knife and it was lunging toward me. I could actually hear myself scream as I frantically turned, ran past the elevator, and entered the staircase with the long butcher knife in close pursuit. I ran down ten flights taking two to three steps at a time. I reached the lobby and continued running straight through both sets of glass doors, up East 31st Street, then up Madison Avenue and did not stop until I reached a patrol car three blocks north.

I explained my situation to them and they drove me back to the hotel. We did not see Mrs. Wright on the ride back to the hotel, outside the hotel, or in the lobby. I took the cops up to her room and sure enough, she answered the door in her shroud. I wondered what she had done with that butcher knife. After speaking with the *lady in white* for a few minutes, it became very apparent that she had some mental problems. Our new guest was checked out of The Roger Williams Hotel and into Bellevue Psychiatric Hospital. Even though Mrs. Wright was only in the hotel for a few hours, she certainly made the list as a guest in my asylum.

I don't want to imply that each day at The Roger Williams was fraught with ominous danger. It is just that I wanted to impress upon you, the reader, that it was not all fun and games. My days were filled with many humorous incidents as well as the sad ones, which encompassed suicides, murder mysteries and other situations that gave me eventful challenges. Truthfully, my family always preferred that I relate the bizarre and silly ones so I think it is time for a change of pace.

DATE WITH THE GOVERNOR - ROOM 1407

Amelia Fineman, another asylum inmate, would certainly be representative of the bizarre and silly. She had been living in the hotel for what seemed like forever and occupied Room 1407. None of the workers could remember a time prior to her arrival. Anyone describing Amelia would be found to use words such as eccentric, odd or strange. To the best of our knowledge she was a divorced woman. We assumed that her ex-husband was paying handsomely, to keep her far away from him, as well as away from Creedmoor Psychiatric Center.

During my first few months at the hotel, I gradually became more familiar with Mrs. Fineman. Amelia was a rather unattractive, huge woman who stood approximately 5' 9" and was grotesquely obese. She probably weighed in excess of 350 pounds. She always wore extremely heavy make-up that made her appear clownish. For example: her rouge was a deep shade of red and looked like big round patches on her cheeks, dark blue eye shadow covered her entire lids and bright orange lipstick seemed to cover not only her lips but also the lower part of her face.

In addition to her unusual appearance, she possessed some truly eccentric habits. She was on the mailing list for what seemed to be every mail-order catalogue printed and it appeared as though she purchased just about every mail-order item available. Amelia's room was wall-to-wall and floor-to-ceiling boxes; there were empty boxes, partially opened boxes and unopened boxes. The room was so cluttered that it was actually impossible to provide her with maid service. The only area of her room devoid of boxes was her bathroom. How this huge woman managed to move around in that small, congested room is still a mystery and she was practically always in her room.

Amelia's phone habits were also a bit unusual. In addition to the provided hotel phone she also had a private phone. Oddly enough her hotel phone was always ringing. This seemed strange because she was not a gregarious, social woman. As long as I could remember Amelia never received any visitors. It was puzzling that she had so many telephone callers.

I recall once mentioning this to my mother. Mom then took it upon herself to start listening in on Amelia's telephone conversations and simultaneously availing herself of some free entertainment. In those days, the switchboard could be set to allow such an intrusion. What Mom heard was intriguing—every one of Amelia's callers had the same voice, different names, but the same voice. Even more fascinating was that they also had the same voice as Amelia.

What actually was going on was this: while Mrs. Fineman sat in her room she would make phone calls from her private phone to the hotel and then ask to be connected to Mrs. Fineman. She would then actually carry on full conversations with herself. As time went on, her callers became more and more high profile (according to my mother). Amelia was clearly trying to impress someone; I'm not sure if it was the hotel employees or herself.

One afternoon she called the switchboard introducing herself as Governor Rockefeller's assistant. After being connected to Mrs. Fineman's room, the assistant proceeded to arrange a dinner date between Amelia and the Governor. The arrangements were that he would pick her up, by helicopter, from the roof of the hotel at 6 P.M.

A few hours later I was standing in the lobby, speaking with Lincoln, when the elevator doors opened. We both looked up and were shocked to see Amelia walk out *all dolled up*. Her idea of dolled up was enough to make a man swear off dating forever! Amelia was beaming with joy and anticipation.

"I'm so excited!" she exclaimed. "I have a dinner date with Governor Rockefeller and he is picking me up with his helicopter. I have to go up to the roof now."

She then went back into the elevator and the door closed. Lincoln and I stood dumbfounded in the lobby watching the floors tick away on the elevator monitor. Sure enough, she took the elevator up to the sixteenth floor. Since it did not descend back to the fourteenth, it is possible that Amelia somehow dragged her huge body up the next flight of stairs to the roof ... to meet her esteemed dinner date. I doubt if this charade was done for our benefit; I believe it occurred because of her delusional state. But then again I'm not half-a-psychiatrist. I still wonder if Mrs. Fineman spent hours on the roof waiting for her date or if she left in tears a little after 6 P.M. In any event, no further word was ever mentioned about her date with the Governor.

THE FAT LADY IN THE TUB - ROOM 1407

One morning, a few weeks later, a guest on the fourteenth floor buzzed the switchboard. "Call the police! Someone is being attacked!" the person said frantically.

Immediately after that, the switchboard lit up from other people on the fourteenth floor. There were reports of screams, whimpers and cries for help. All the calls were demanding that Mom call the police. Mom called me instead; she knew we tried to avoid calling the police unless it was absolutely necessary. I grabbed Lincoln and both of us ran into the service elevator.

We rushed up to the fourteenth floor to see for ourselves what was causing so much turmoil. The screams were coming from room 1407. As we neared Amelia's room the frenzied screams for help got louder. Assuming that she couldn't get to the door I used my passkey to unlock and open the door. Bumping into cartons of mail-order rubbish we followed the cries. No sign of her yet. The cries led us toward the bathroom.

Rushing into the bathroom we saw her. There she was, naked ... in the tub, lying on her back, in about one inch of water. **What a sight to behold**. Even though she resembled a wounded hippo, she actually she did not appear to be injured. From the position she was in, I assumed she hadn't accidentally fallen in. Evidently, Amelia had managed to squeeze her large body into the tub and now could not move a muscle to get herself out. The poor woman was really suffering. We had to get her out of there. Lincoln and I sprang into action. He grabbed her left arm, and I reached over and grabbed her right.

"One, two, three pull!" I instructed. We couldn't budge her. Again I called out, "One, two, three, pull!"

We couldn't maneuver her and realized that we had to summon help. Speaking softly in what I hoped was an assuring voice, I told Amelia to try and remain calm while we went to get assistance. Lincoln and I then raced to the elevator.

This was the perfect job for Ernie. HIS muscular strength surely would be enough to get her out. He was stronger than all the rest of us put together. We found Ernie in his basement shop; I explained the situation to him and instructed him to quickly go to Amelia's room and get her out of the tub. I felt confident that the crisis would quickly and successfully be resolved. Lincoln and I returned to the front desk and tried to calm down.

Fifteen minutes later the switchboard started buzzing again from the fourteenth floor.

One caller screamed, "Get help!"

Another caller yelled, "It sounds like two people are being killed!"

Fearfully, Lincoln and I took the service elevator back up to the fourteenth floor. As soon as the elevator door opened we heard the screams. This time, however, they didn't sound quite the same. Tearing into Amelia's bathroom, both Lincoln and I stopped short upon witnessing the sight. We looked at each other, and then we both began to laugh so hard that I was literally afraid I'd wet my pants. Try to picture this ... Amelia was now face down in the tub with her huge, huge rear end facing up to greet us. Ernie was hardly visible—he was practically hidden beneath her.

We heard him grumble in a very muffled voice, "Stop your fuckin' laughin' and get me out of here. I can hardly breathe!"

When I stopped laughing enough to be able to talk, I went to Amelia's hotel phone and called the fire department. By this time, we were on a first name basis because of our many calls for assistance. The fire department would be there soon. In the meantime, Ernie would have to wait, lying under Mrs. Fineman's naked body. What some guys wouldn't do to be in this position.

Once again our fearless friends saved the day and then Ernie was able to explain what had happened. While Ernie was trying to lift Amelia up by her arms, he lost his footing in the tub. He slipped and before he knew it, there he was with Amelia's large, naked body on top of him.

* * *

I recently discovered that these events are not unique. Not long after writing this segment, I saw an Internet blog in which a young woman was describing a funny story that a policeman relative had recounted to her. Apparently this policeman received a call to rescue a fat lady from a tub. He thought the obese woman was trapped in the tub because of a suction effect that occurred when the water was released. In his rescue they used olive oil and muscle to save her. Had I known this earlier, I would have added olive oil to my other emergency equipment.

FIRE ON THE 14ᵀᴴ FLOOR - ROOM 1407

I t would not take long for Amelia to avail herself of her saviors again. A few months later, while attempting to refill her butane cigarette lighter, she set her room ablaze. The hotel was built as a fireproof structure with heavy metal entry doors for each room so that most fires would be confined to the unit, as long as the doors and windows remained shut. Amelia fled from her room without attempting to extinguish what was initially a very minor fire, thus, allowing the flames to spread and consume her room.

While she frantically waddled up and down the corridor yelling, **"Help, help, somebody get help,"** her treasured purchases were being destroyed.

With all the potential fuel present in her room, a significant fire developed.

The corridor filled with heavy smoke while her ponderous body struggled to find the energy to continue scurrying to and fro pleading, **"Please, please, help, please!"**

Of course, our switchboard was all lit up again, this time with alarmed guests calling for the fire department. I think the department probably set up an annex next to our building, because they were here in a few minutes and extinguished the fire just as quickly. As I assessed the damage, I was elated to discover that there was no damage to any of the surrounding rooms.

However, there were other losses. One permanent guest lost two cats that she was never reunited with. A Japanese transient guest, in a panic, threw his wallet out the window. I really can't explain what he could have been thinking. He, too, was never reunited with his lost belongings. Mrs. Fineman lost all her mail-order merchandise, opened, partially opened or never opened. I had handymen carry the refuse to the basement and suggested to Amelia that she might wish to search through the rubbish and perhaps salvage some things.

She exclaimed with great enthusiasm, "No, thank you. I'll just reorder."

I, of course, did look through the carnage. Curiosity got the best of me. Amazingly, there was one large unopened carton that escaped damage. Opening the box I found it filled with crystal bottles of Shalimar Perfume. Annette, to this present day, still has not depleted this cache.

BENEVOLENT MAN OF THE CLOTH - ROOM 209

The white, stretch limousine pulled up into our loading zone, and a uniformed chauffeur opened the passenger door for our potential new guest. A young (thirty to forty year old) man emerged and headed into our lobby. He was a six-footer, dressed in a conservatively cut dark suit, sporting a mustache, and closely cropped hair. He smiled as he introduced himself as Father Flynn. Father Flynn was a well-spoken black who had a slight southern drawl. His sentences emerged in bullet point phrases—as if he were giving a sermon or perhaps lecturing a college class. His face continually maintained a warm, friendly smile as he inquired about our accommodations and the security of the hotel and surrounding area.

I proudly explained to Father Flynn that all of our rooms had private bathrooms with tub and shower and practically all of them had kitchenettes. I described our rate structure and maid services and pointed out the conveniences of some of our neighboring establishments. While doing so, I tried to assure him that he would be safe both in the hotel and its immediate vicinity.

"Mr. Sokol, is it? Ah don't require cookin' facilities. Sir, ah just needs a clean, quiet room for mah contemplation."

"I understand," I said wondering what it was he would be contemplating. Our hotel had four units without kitchenettes, 209, 210, 309, and 310. Miss. Flanagan, the housekeeper, used both third floor rooms (one to sleep in and the other as a closet). That left 209 and 210. Both of these rooms overlooked the alley, offered a scenic view of a brick wall, and were dark and depressing. Considering their small dimensions they were virtually not rentable. I thought, why not take a chance and show him one of these rooms.

"Father Flynn, follow me and let me show you some accommodations."

I led him to the service elevator and took him to the second floor.

"Verah nice carpeting ... hmm, a quiet floor, too," he remarked in a soothing tone of voice.

I was embarrassed to open the door to room 209, but ... what the heck.

As I led him into the room, he exclaimed, "Purrfect, purrfect. This would be ahdeel for mah purposes, and mah furniture will fit right in."

I ran a hotel, not an apartment house, but if he was willing to rent room 209, I would be happy to carry the existing furniture out myself. Father Flynn moved in that evening. His furniture arrived the following day. The delivery consisted of two odd shaped brass table lamps, a small walnut laminated kneehole desk, and a low, revolving orange tub chair. To achieve the right spiritual aura, he had requested that we remove the bulbs from the ceiling fixture. With just the two lamps and very little natural light, room 209 took on an even eerier look than usual. Surprisingly, he instructed the housekeeper to supply maid service only once weekly but to change his towels daily.

Any of the staff that met or interacted with Father Flynn described him as soft- spoken, polite, considerate and well-mannered. His bills were paid promptly, in cash, every week. He was cordial to everyone and as far as I was concerned it was delightful to have such a model guest; especially since he was such a welcomed departure from my asylum guests.

Father Flynn projected the image of a man of the cloth, yet, despite the presence of a Bible resting on his desk, I did not have any inkling as to what religious group he was affiliated with. During our chance encounters in the lobby our conversations were never steered in the direction of prayers, sermons or other religious activities.

I am not certain when I started to become aware of some curious oddities. It was probably around three weeks after his arrival that Father Flynn would stop by the front desk everyday and request that we cash a few $25 and $50 denomination money orders. At first we accommodated him. As the days went on, his cash needs grew to between $200 and $400 per day. This was now becoming too much for our small register.

I contacted him, informed him of our concerns, and suggested he utilize the local Chase Bank for his cash needs. He graciously came into my office and reiterated his appreciation of our hospitality and said he would subsequently cash his money orders at the bank. I thanked him and asked if there was anything else I could do to further enhance his stay at The Roger Williams Hotel.

He smiled and responded, "No, but thank ya fur askin."

The following week he started to have visitors. At first there were two or three a day and then the number accelerated to between ten and fifteen. I started to wonder and also worry a little ... was he giving marriage counseling? Was he sermonizing in his tiny room? Then, one day, a guest of his forgot his copy of the *Amsterdam Harlem News* at the front desk. The newspaper was open to what appeared to be an advertisement. This is what I read:

I, Father Flynn,
DOUBLE GUARANTEE
TO ENDEAVOR
to resolve each and every
problem you might have
Call
MU 9-0600 Ext. 209

Well, that explained the traffic. His visitors, followers and parishioners were certainly well-mannered and had created no extra demands on my staff. I prayed that he should be well and be able to continue to serve his congregation.

Two weeks later the hotel had surprise visitors. Three tall, clean-cut young men dressed in very conservative, navy blue business suits approached our front desk.

Mom was at the switchboard and I was behind the desk. Flashing badges they burst into the front office.

One, in a strong, almost threatening tone said to Mom, "Back away from the switchboard and stand against the wall!"

She jumped up and quickly obliged.

Another man turned toward me and inquired, "Is the guest occupying room 209 in?"

I responded with, "Look, I haven't got the foggiest notion what the problem is or who you are"

"We are the FBI!" said the third man, giving me a second and closer look at his Federal Agency badge.

The agent next to Mom in a firm voice said, "Go back to the switchboard and ring room 209. If he is in, tell him there is a woman in the lobby requesting to see him."

Mom obeyed. She rang the room and informed her FBI agent that there was no answer.

One of the other two agents then requested that I take them up to Father Flynn's room. I wasn't sure if I had the legal authority to do this. They had showed me no warrant, but they certainly had me intimidated enough. So while Mom stayed with her agent, I went into the elevator with my two Feds. We took the elevator to the second floor and proceeded to enter room 209. The room was bathed in its eerie illumination, yet enough light was emitted to clearly see that Father Flynn had no clothing in the closet. Aside from his ever-present bible, and his furniture, he had no personal possessions at all. After a few minutes, they were ready to return to the lobby. I was getting more and more uncomfortable and nervous. I sensed that they suspected that if Mom were given the chance she would try to alert Father Flynn. Without saying so, they gave me the impression that they may have even thought that we were all complicit in whatever misdeeds they suspected Father Flynn had committed. Mom was allowed to continue working the board but under the watchful eye of the agent assigned to her. The other two took up strategic positions in our lobby.

One hour later, Father Flynn entered the lobby to the shouts of, "**FREEZE! Put your hands up. You are under arrest.**"

WITNESS FOR THE PROSECUTION

In my naivety, I wondered if Father Flynn was embezzling church funds. My jolt to reality occurred a few months later. One morning I received a letter summoning me to Detroit, Michigan to appear as a witness for the prosecution of Father Flynn, a.k.a. ... I have no recollection of his true name. The government, with surprising efficiency, had not only prepaid my flights to and from Detroit, but also for my room at the Sheraton Cadillac—a *real* hotel. I couldn't wait to get home and show Annette my letter.

She thought this was very exciting. Her husband was summoned to be a witness at a trial. However, she admitted that she wasn't very happy about being separated from me for the first time since our marriage almost five years ago; I was uneasy leaving her with two little ones. Yes, we were now the proud parents of two wonderful girls. Our younger daughter, Jodi, was born in May 1962 and Sharyn was now two. We also moved from a three-room apartment to a four-room apartment on the same floor. My in-laws rented our original apartment. If there should be a problem while I was gone, knowing that my in-laws lived practically next door, gave me peace of mind.

So off I went to Detroit—I had no choice. Flying alone was going to be a new experience for me. Not only had I never flown alone before, but also to be candid, the only flights I had ever taken at that stage of my life, was our honeymoon trip to Florida.

I still had no idea what crimes Father Flynn had committed, or what was expected of me, but I figured that this would prove to be a very exciting trip. Going to Detroit should be interesting since I had never been there before, and I certainly had never been a witness for the government or anyone else for that matter. Nevertheless, I was having very mixed feelings; on one hand I was feeling very important while at the same time feeling nervous and anxious.

My flight to Detroit was uneventful. I took a cab to the Sheraton Cadillac Hotel and checked in. The Sheraton Cadillac was a very luxurious hotel in comparison to The Roger Williams Hotel. It had an enormous lobby with shiny, marble floors, large crystal chandeliers, numerous sofas and chairs, and lots of people milling about. There was even a dual escalator. Four people worked behind the check-in desk. I tried to imagine the payroll in this hotel; it had to be enormous.

The bellman took me to my room and pointed out the amenities to me. The accommodations were even more luxurious than I had anticipated. The room was very large with plush beige carpeting, Italian style furniture made of a rich, dark wood. The beautiful striped draperies coordinated with the floral bedspread. The bathroom was also very up to date ... there was even a little straw basket holding shampoo, conditioner, soaps, a shower cap, a shoeshine kit and a sewing kit.

We certainly didn't supply these things at The Roger Williams Hotel!

As the bellman was leaving, a red light started blinking on the telephone. The bellman informed me that I must have a message and that I should call the telephone operator. Sure enough, there was a message for me from Miss. Arlene Richards, the Federal Prosecutor, asking me to meet her at her office at 9 A.M the following morning.

I realized I hadn't eaten dinner yet and I was getting very hungry. Since the government was also paying for my meals, I figured I might as well treat myself well. I went down to the hotel restaurant and ordered a martini. While sipping my drink, I ordered dinner. For an appetizer I had a shrimp cocktail, which consisted of four very large shrimp sitting in a glass bowl atop a bed of crisp lettuce. I could smell the delicious aroma of my steak before I could even see it. The T-bone was smothered in butter and accompanied by a baked potato loaded with sour cream and chives. For dessert I had hot apple pie a la mode. The ice cream meandered in small streams over the sides of the pie. I ended this superb meal with a cup of piping hot coffee and felt extremely satisfied. Afterwards, I went back to my room, watched some television and soon fell sound asleep.

The next morning I returned to the restaurant and ordered a large orange juice, pancakes with a side of bacon, coffee and a cheese Danish. This restaurant was really good. The orange juice was fresh-squeezed, the pancakes were hot and fluffy, and the bacon was crisp. This was starting to feel great. Perhaps, I could become a professional witness.

It was 8:20 A.M. and time for me to leave. I had to get to my appointment by 9 A.M.; I wouldn't dare to be late for the prosecutor. I asked one of the four desk clerks for the best way to get to the address that I had for Miss. Richards' office. It was only a few blocks away and since it was such a warm, sunny fall morning, I decided to take a leisurely walk. I arrived at the office building at 8:45 A.M, took the elevator up to the fifth floor and proceeded to suite 502.

At exactly 9 A.M, I was ushered into Miss. Arlene Richards' office. Miss. Richards was curt, efficient, and full of herself. She asked about the money orders and the visitors. I told her what I knew. I finally found out that Father Flynn was indicted for wire fraud and ten other felony charges. Miss. Richards also showed me the advertisement that I had already seen when it originally appeared in the <u>Amsterdam Harlem News</u>. To this day, I still believe it was a brilliant ad. All he did was promise to "try" to help people overcome their difficulties.

What I discovered, however, was that Father Flynn promised callers that upon praying in his bible, he would note what psalm or prayer he was reading and give them the page or paragraph number. This number was sold to his *parishioners* for $25 and $50. He actually was promising to give them the next winning lottery number. I could not believe that people could be so naïve. But, I guess, desperation and poverty lead people to do desperate things. I strongly believe his callers acted not out of greed but in the best interests of their families. Perhaps, I was the naïve one.

Miss. Richards then walked me through a list of questions that she believed I would be asked and told me how she wanted me to answer them. I took exception to having words put in my mouth and told her so. However, she continued with her questions and again told me what my responses should be. I found this extremely upsetting. If my corroboration of Father Flynn's activities at The Roger Williams Hotel resulted in his conviction, so be it, but I refused to be a party to half-truths and fabrication.

The next day, I was called in as a witness. As I approached the stand, Father Flynn jumped up with his familiar smile and gave me a cordial hello. The prosecutor was not pleased with my testimony; I may have even been deemed a hostile witness. Subsequently, I learned that the good "Father" was convicted and given a stiff federal sentence. I was no longer an innocent; my naïvety was lost. Going forward, I promised myself that I would scrutinize all who appeared before me and never accept things at face value.

Naïvety 201

I thought that I had lost my naïvety but later discovered that only by suffering through some embarrassing and at times costly situations, does a true awakening occur and bring meaningful knowledge beyond the Bachelor's Degree. The next two incidents clearly confirm this.

It became necessary to start purchasing window air conditioners to replace the antiquated ones that were currently being used. However, the procurement process was beginning to be a strain on the hotel's budget. Across from the hotel was an appliance store that I had not previously sourced, so I thought it might be appropriate to get a few quotes from a neighbor. Their prices turned out to be no better than the quotes that I had received elsewhere.

I returned directly to the hotel and no sooner did I enter the front office than a young gentleman called out to me, "Excuse me, weren't you just in our store asking about buying six air conditioning units?"

"Yes, I was. Did I leave something there?"

He smiled and said, "No, not at all. I am John Nash and perhaps we **can** resolve your needs after all. We have six units that were prepaid for by a customer who ended up going bankrupt. They're last year's model but they are all in the original cartons. You can have them for $400 but it would have to be a cash deal."

It sounded good to me. "Let me get the cash, and I'll walk back with you."

I got the cash from the hotel safe and then the two of us walked across the street.

As we approached the front door he said, "Give me the money, I'll make out the receipt and meet you at the side entrance with one of my men, a hand truck, and the six units. Just give me five minutes."

I thought ... this is truly was a good deal. After standing at the side entrance for twenty minutes, I walked back to the front entrance, went into the store and started to look for John. He wasn't immediately visible, so I approached one of the salesmen and asked for him.

"Pardon me, could you tell John that I'm still waiting for him."

"Excuse me, who are you looking for?"

"John ... John Nash."

"I'm sorry, we have no one by that name working here."

How long does it take for someone to realize that he has been taken? In my case, the flash of light went off with the end of the Nash syllable. Since I was too embarrassed to speak to the manager, I just slinked my way out of the store. I still can't believe the lengths that some people would go to set up a sting operation. In any event, I had now finished the second of my postgraduate credits in naivety.

* * *

Many vendors walked through our front doors pitching their wares. Some had stolen or counterfeit watches and many others appeared with a plethora of assorted merchandise. All of these vendors were quickly escorted out the door. One day when I was momentarily covering the front desk, a gentleman came in carrying what appeared to be a bolt of cloth. He introduced himself as Sheldon Jacobs and claimed to be in the textile business.

" Here," he said, "feel this material."

I reached out and felt the cloth.

"Smooth like a baby's ass, huh?"

To me it didn't feel like a baby's ass, it actually felt more like what I imagined cashmere would feel like.

"Is this cashmere?" I asked.

"Sir, this is *suit material* ... finest textile made! You don't make a suit from cashmere."

"What would I do with it?"

"There is more than enough material here to have a suit made for you. You can have this bolt for $8 and probably have a tailor custom design a suit for you for another $50."

I carried the bolt over to my mother and had her feel the material. She couldn't get over its softness.

"It's feels great but would you wear a green suit?" Mom asked.

"It's not a bright green, it's a deep grayish green. It would be perfect."

I gave Mr. Jacobs $8 and the following day brought the bolt of cloth over to Bonne Cleaners on East 34th Street. Mr. William Kremer, the owner, employed Izzie Cooper, a tailor who was reputed to be a true craftsman.

I showed Izzie the bolt of material and he thought it would be excellent for a suit. He measured me and two weeks later I brought home my new suit.

Annette touched the material and exclaimed, "This really feels smooth and I love the color. Try it on; I can't wait to see how it fits you."

After I put the suit on Annette sounded really excited, " It really fits great! That tailor did a fantastic job; it actually looks like a very expensive suit. It's a shame that you can't always have your suits custom-made."

The next day I proudly walked into the hotel wearing my new attire. All during my working hours, I took painstaking care not to soil the garment. Even though the suit wasn't made from magic cloth, I certainly felt great wearing it ... and I *really* loved the feeling of the fabric.

I left the hotel at 6 P.M. and walked uptown on Madison Avenue to catch the express bus to the Bronx. About two blocks from the bus stop, there was a sudden downpour. Since I had no umbrella or raincoat, I began to run. Fortunately, the bus was waiting at the stop but I was already drenched. The rain stopped pretty soon thereafter but a little too late for me.

About ten minutes from home I started to experience pain in the groin area. I was somewhat concerned, even though I was accustomed to aches and pains due to the physical labor I exerted in the hotel, this particular pain was a new one for me. I couldn't wait to get off the bus, go home and lie down. As we were approaching the Sedgwick Avenue stop I bent down to pick up my attaché case. My shirtsleeves were sticking out from my suit jacket but I really didn't give it much thought. As I got off the bus I felt a cool draft on my ankles. I looked down and saw my wet pant legs were clinging to me. I had no patience for this; I really needed to get home! **The pain in the groin was really bothering me.**

As I entered our apartment I heard Annette gasp and then start to laugh hysterically. She couldn't control herself! I quickly learned that my suit had shrunk three inches in length. The good news was that my groin pain was caused by the shrinkage of cloth and not from some other, more horrible reason. The other good news was that I had now, *finally*, completed my postgraduate courses in naïvety.

THE WATER TANK

Managing a Manhattan midtown hotel might seem glamorous to you but many of my responsibilities were fairly mundane and some ... simply disgusting. Just think, 216 rooms add up to 216 toilets. Need I say any more on the subject?

When the engineer was not available to handle certain repairs, the responsibility fell on my narrow shoulders. Therefore, over time, I learned more than I ever wanted to know about water pipes, water pumps and water tanks.

Growing up in Brooklyn, one could turn on a faucet and miraculously water would appear. I had heard about water main breaks in Manhattan and the inherent havoc and disruption they created. However, I never had the desire to learn specifics about the subject.

What I learned during my on-the-job training at the hotel was that to feed a sixteen-story structure, water pumps were needed to take the water from street level to a storage tank on the roof. From the tank, the water was gravity-fed to the rooms. Our hotel had two powerful pumps in the basement to accomplish this task. One pump was always in use while the other served as a back up.

Perched on the roof, upon steel girders that stretched two stories above our sixteenth floor, was our water tank. I suspect that for economical reasons and for a shorter on-site construction time, this tank was made of a timber wood design as opposed to steel or concrete. Basically it was made using tongue and groove staves that were held together with galvanized steel cables. The life expectancy of the timber wood design, supposedly, equaled those of the other materials. Inside the tank was a pine wood deck and on the top was a conical shaped roof with an access door. Now you know more than you ever needed to know about water tanks and definitely more than *our engineer*.

* * *

Ernie, The Engineer (Janitor/Superintendent), was a man who always spoke with authority. He projected himself as an expert in his field whether working on elevator repairs, boiler problems or any other of his odd jobs. As I mentioned previously, since we had a tight budget, I had to assist Ernie with many of the recurring repair problems such as refrigerators, air conditioners, televisions and the dreaded toilets. Eventually, I even learned to make many of these repairs myself.

With my infinitesimal knowledge, I would entrust the most complicated maintenance and repair work to Ernie's capable hands. I greatly admired his dedication. He would even offer to come back to the hotel after work hours to do major repair jobs. I appreciated his thoughtfulness and work ethics. Ernie was a solid trooper. By coming in at night, he was forced to make repairs without either my or any other staff member's assistance.

* * *

Many mornings when I arrived at work, I would be greeted with a barrage of complaints from tenants and guests. I thought it peculiar that they complained of spending hours with no hot water, and sometimes no water at all—when to my knowledge, there were never any major leaks or pump breakdowns at such times. What I discovered much later was, *surprise,* Ernie possessed only a rudimentary knowledge of anything.

I was finally keyed into Ernie's shortcomings, one day, when a major water leak developed mid-afternoon. Upon learning of the leak I, of course, immediately ran in search of Ernie.

Finding him busy in his basement shop, I yelled, "Ernie, hurry, I need your assistance! We have a bad leak on the ninth floor!"

"Don't worry, Boss, I'll handle it later this evening."

"Ernie, you don't understand, this is a major one! It looks as if it could wash the entire hotel down Madison Avenue!"

I felt incredibly anxious as I grabbed Ernie and ran to investigate the source of the leak. From my earlier description, you learned that water reaches the rooms by gravity-feed. What I didn't mention was that each room had hot and cold water valves, thus enabling an individual room's water supply to be disconnected from the building's system during repairs. In this way there would be no disruption of water supply to the other rooms. If the room valves malfunctioned, there were additional safety valves on the sixteenth floor that would enable us to shut down an entire vertical line i.e., rooms 203, 303, 403, etc. On this particular day, we discovered that the leak originated in room 910, and as luck would have it, the respective valves in this unit did not hold.

"Damn it, let's go Ernie! We've got to shut the entire 'ten' line!"

We ran to the elevator, went up to the sixteenth floor, and tried to shut the "ten" line valves. They spun endlessly; they did not hold. In mindless desperation, I randomly tried the valves for the other individual lines. None of them worked!

"Ernie, what the fuck is going on?"

Ernie gave me a dumbfounded expression; he was equally as baffled. I was beginning to panic when Ernie suddenly took control of the situation.

"I have a great idea that will work, Boss. Let's drain the water tank!"

Before we could drain the water tank, we would have to shut the power to the pumps. So we raced back to the elevator, down to the basement, and shut off the pumps. Then we took the elevator to the sixteenth floor again, and quickly ran up the stairs to the roof. Ernie was first to locate the large drain valve under the water tank. He opened it and the water started draining out of the tank. What a great idea! Devoid of water pressure and water in the pipes we were able to fix the breach in our water line. **Thank God for Ernie**!

Later that day, I spent a great deal of time rehashing and investigating what could have caused the faulty valves. Finally, I realized that Ernie had only been going through the motions with me. He knew none of the valves would work. He knew because his neglect and mishandling over the years had destroyed them one by one. Therefore, the only possible way to make these repairs was to drain the water tank, and that's what he had been doing. Ernie made these repairs at night so that no one would discover his inadequacies. Now, I understood the countless complaints I was getting concerning lack of water service during the nights.

I am embarrassed to admit, however, that we continued to do our plumbing repairs the way Ernie had been doing them all along. To call in an outside contractor to fix all the valves, would have entailed a steep repair bill. More importantly, it would have been an admission of my own incompetence to the investment partners. This was really scary; I was starting to think and act like Ernie.

* * *

Months later another major leak developed. Ernie and I instinctively shut the pumps, raced to the roof, and started to drain the tank. Looking back at the matter-of-fact way we did this is in itself, pretty humorous. In any event, I left Ernie in complete control at the tank and returned to my office. Sometime later, a call came in from housekeeping looking for Ernie. They needed his assistance with something or other. I called Ernie's shop ... no answer. I had Lincoln search for him, to no avail. If Lincoln, who knew all Ernie's hiding places couldn't find him, something was awry.

Could he still be on the roof? I figured it couldn't hurt to check up there ... perhaps he was still working on the tank—no sign of Ernie. Suddenly, I had a horrible premonition. No, it can't be, no way. I looked up at the two-story steel ladder that gives one access to the tank. Now, I am reluctant to admit this, but I am terrified of heights; you could not get me near the edge of a roof for all the money in the world.

So I stood in the middle of the roof yelling, "ERNIE, ERNIE! Where are you? Are you okay?"

I heard a faint cry, *"Help! Help!"*

I was so happy to hear his voice. Like many of the other crazy things I found myself doing in that hotel, I was suddenly climbing the ladder. I ascended gripping each rung so tightly that my hands were starting to cramp and sweat. Over and over again I kept hearing his cries for help. I continued to force myself upwards.

To Ernie I shouted, "I'm coming! I'm coming!"

To myself I whispered, *"Don't look down ... don't look down."*

It seemed like an eternity before I reached the top. The door to the tank was opened which enabled me to peer inside. There he was—thrashing about in the water trying to keep afloat! He was accompanied by pieces of wood, unfortunately none of which were large enough to give him any support.

I yelled out to Ernie, "I'm going to get help. Just keep swimming!" Who knows how long he had been doggy paddling in the tank; I had to get help fast! I don't remember how I descended, but I do know it was mindless and quick. I ran into the closest room on the sixteenth floor and called for the "New York City Fire Department". Once again they responded quickly and managed to fish Ernie out of the tank in one piece. The good news was the pump was working, the guests had water again, and Ernie was visibly unharmed.

Later Ernie explained what had happened. He had fixed the leak and went down to turn on the water pump. Nothing happened. He then switched the back-up pump on. Again, nothing happened. I must give him credit for logically determining that the pumps were not getting the signal to turn on. He then proceeded to return to the water tank surmising that the float in the tank must be hung up. This would prevent the tank from refilling. So Ernie climbed out onto the wood platform to clear the jamb on the float switch. Unfortunately for him, just as he cleared the jamb, the rotted wood platform cracked and gave in. Regrettably, he left the power on for the pump, so it started to refill the tank causing Ernie to end up playing fish for quite awhile.

* * *

Writing about Ernie, just got me thinking about how interesting it is to note how individuals address each other in a business setting. At the Roger Williams, invariably, I used the surname. Hulet Lincoln was called Lincoln, Orson Mack was Mack, and Mary Flannigan was Mrs. Flannigan. There were, however, exceptions to this rule. Pepe was Pepe and Ernie was Ernie. Pepe's last name was Gomez, and somehow, I cannot even recall Ernie's last name, which is just as well ... to me he will always be Ernie.

As incompetent as he was, I had become dependant upon Ernie. Even though I suspected he concealed his "entrepreneurial" skills and could also be devious at times, a close relationship developed between us. Our closeness extended to include our families. One day Ernie invited my daughter and me for a day of fishing at an upstate reservoir. Fishing was the only area where Ernie truly displayed some degree of expertise and knowledge. It turned out to be an exciting day. Sharyn was thoroughly immersed in the challenge of landing a fish without ever touching those *icky* worms, and Ernie was trying hard to stay dry and not join the fish. Over the years, Annette and I took his two children together with our children to the circus and the ice shows at Madison Square Garden. We all enjoyed spending time together.

MURDER AT THE ROGER WILLIAMS HOTEL

As close as Ernie and I were, that is how opposite his relationship with Mack was. Mack despised and hated Ernie, and the feeling was mutual. For some unknown reason they hated each other with a vengeance. I thought about it often, almost daily, actually. It was imperative to maintain some degree of harmony between my employees and to quickly be able to address any catalyst that would disrupt it. Try as I did, I was unable to get these two to be civil to each other. The best I could hope for was an existence that would not include physical harm to either of them.

It was never substantiated, but I believed that Mack was consumed with jealousy and envy. Here was a man adept in carpentry, furniture repair, carpet laying, painting, locksmithing and some electrical work. At least he understood the concepts of electricity enough to avoid electrocution, or worse yet, burning down the hotel. He had the capacity to learn and become proficient in all disciplines required to maintain the hotel. So here he was, forced to see Ernie, pompously expounding on his knowledge and ability in everything. Mack could easily see through his deceit. The bottom line, I believe, was Mack was jealous that Ernie was the Engineer and he remained at the lower handyman level.

One afternoon, Miss. Flanagan, the Housekeeper, called me and excitedly exclaimed, "Ernie and Mack are fighting again! They are in the basement."

I asked Lincoln to go with me. We took the service elevator to the basement. Before the doors even opened, we could hear the loud threatening exchanges between them. As we approached them, the intensity of their dispute was raised a notch or two and they started to push and shove each other.

Before the ensuing blows could follow, I screamed, **"Cut this shit out—are you both nuts?** If you have personal things to iron out please do it on your own time and outside this building. Union or no union, if you guys persist in this crap you're both out of here!"

Peace slowly returned to the basement and, with a deep sigh, I returned to my office. I couldn't dislodge the sight of their fight from my mind and spent the rest of the day wrestling with possible, palatable solutions to their never ending feuding. As with many other hotel problems, this one resolved itself.

* * *

The next morning, at 8:45 A.M., I received a call from Mrs. Mack asking to speak to her husband. I asked her to hold and buzzed Miss. Flanagan from another line. I was informed that Mack had not shown up for work today. Getting back to Mrs. Mack's line I told her that her husband had not come into work this morning. She immediately burst into tears, "Orson didn't come home last night and this has never happened before" she sobbed.

I assured her that I would make inquiries and get back to her as soon as possible. I then contacted Miss. Flanagan and informed her that I was calling a meeting for 10 A.M. Aside from Bella and the desk clerk, everyone was required to attend. In a small environment such as The Roger Williams Hotel word spread quickly through the corridors and rooms. By the time I appeared downstairs, everyone was standing together demonstrating group solidarity ... except for Ernie. He was standing off in a corner by himself. Every so often, someone from the group would pass an accusatory glance in his direction. When he caught their eye, they would immediately turn away.

I wasn't wearing a detective's outfit, but in my opinion, I still managed to pose intelligent, cogent, rational thought-provoking questions. One by one they each claimed they had not seen Mack after the fight. No one saw him leave either. Ernie was curiously defensive in his denials. At the end of the meeting, I asked Miss. Flanagan to check all vacant rooms and storage areas. Lincoln and I proceeded to search the basement area. We went into Mack's small shop to search for some evidence of his actions. Everything looked normal except for his homemade workbench being slightly askew. I returned to my office and called Mrs. Mack.

"Mrs. Mack this is Herb Sokol from The Roger Williams Hotel. I am sorry to tell you that that no one has seen Orson since a slight altercation here yesterday. Given it is out of character for Orson not to come home after work, I would strongly urge you to contact the police."

She whispered, "God all mighty," and immediately started crying.

I felt terrible having to give Mrs. Mack such frightening news over the phone. I hoped that in addition to calling the police, she had some good friends or family near her apartment that she could call on for assistance and support.

The next day real detectives appeared in my office. They asked me to give them Orson's work schedule for the day; they also wanted to know if I had observed or heard of any unusual incidents during Orson's last day at work. I briefed them as best as I could and felt obligated to mention the fight between him and Ernie. The detectives then asked to speak to the housekeeper and her staff. The meetings lasted about one hour, after which they performed a cursory search of the premises. After this search, Ernie was asked to join them for discussions at the precinct. He was questioned for two hours. Then the cops wanted to give him a polygraph test. He agreed to do this but the results were inconclusive.

The following morning, the detectives reappeared in my office—one of them said, "There is one area that we overlooked in our search yesterday."

Inquiring as to where that was, the other detective replied, "The boiler room."

I couldn't believe what they were implying. Could Ernie have killed Mack and destroyed the evidence by throwing him into the furnace? They didn't say this; they didn't have to. Their very request certainly implied it. The thought of this was making me sick to my stomach

In the early years of the hotel, Con Edison supplied steam to fill our radiators and to heat our water. Some years back, before I started working at the hotel, the owners converted to an independent power plant. Two oil-fired burners were installed. These units heated water coils in its interior. The subsequent steam that was generated flowed into our radiators and also heated the water in the hot water tanks.

Our oil company supplied technical assistance for any matters that exceeded our expertise and Ernie was responsible for basic maintenance. I'm pretty sure this was the reason that the detectives wanted to examine the fire chambers. So I shut the burners down and after they cooled, the detectives took a probe and started to search for human remains. I am happy to say that they did not find any. But, unfortunately, there was no closure for the missing Mack.

* * *

Later that week Pepe, in a quest to find a replacement trowel for his bent and broken one, entered Mack's shop. He could not locate one on the tool pegboard and proceeded to examine the items on the workbench ... still no luck. Then he bent down and started to remove the cartons from the bottom shelf. As he pulled one of the cartons off the shelf, he fell back in shock. There staring at him was the missing Mack! Mystery solved—the autopsy indicated that Mack died of a massive heart attack. Apparently Mack moved the table so that he could squeeze behind to retrieve something. He then succumbed to a heart attack.

I will always wonder if the heart attack was precipitated by the trauma of the heated argument. However, Ernie was absolved of all responsibility and life continued at The Roger Williams Hotel with Ernie as Chief Engineer.

THE VOLUPTUOUS BLOND - ROOM 208

Previously, I introduced my mom, Bella, as a woman who literally was reborn after starting her new career. To many, running a switchboard could be viewed as a step above working as a factory laborer. To Bella, coming from her previous day job of plucking chicken feathers in the butcher shop, this was an executive position with important responsibilities. She became meticulous about selecting her wardrobe for her office job and looked forward with great anticipation to the start of each new day. Just as I had suddenly been thrust into a strange new world, so had my mom. Working in this hotel, certainly had no resemblance to anything either of us had previously experienced.

Bella was quiet, reserved and projected herself as a sweet, innocent lady. She was a woman who under no circumstance would utter a negative word about anyone, no matter what misdeeds they might have done. If you entrusted her with confidential information, you could be sure she would keep this secret to her death. There was no way to pry anything out of her, including her age, even under the threat of severe consequences. Her demeanor was always at an even level and she was very quick to smile. If you wanted her to giggle, all you had to do was give her one sip of liquor. If you don't believe me, ask Sharyn about the New Year's Eve that Mom, Annette, Sharyn and I spent in Israel.

* * *

My sister, Irene, on the other hand, recently reminded me of an incident, which occurred when we were children that belies all that I have just stated. The five of us still lived in the small three-room walk-up apartment on the third floor. Children being children, we would naturally move about and play with enthusiasm. Being poor, our floors were bare and we pranced about on the hard wooden surface. Mrs. Slotnick, who resided in the apartment beneath us, took exception to our normal daily activities and would take a broom and bang on her ceiling. All she accomplished was to remove chips of paint from her ceiling. Her actions elicited no response from our mother or us.

Then one day, after she probably banged the last bit of paint from her ceiling, she stormed up to our apartment and started screaming, "I can't take the noise from your animals any longer! **You have to stop them,**" and with that said, she stormed down to her apartment.

A transformation took over my mother. She picked up a pot and started smashing it on the radiators and the steam risers. SHE BANGED IT ON THE FLOOR. SHE BANGED IT ON THE WALLS. SHE BANGED IT ON ANY SURFACE THAT WOULD RESOUND WITH A DEAFENING NOISE!

As she banged her pot she kept yelling, "**YOU WANT TO HEAR NOISE, I'LL GIVE YOU NOISE.**"

Five minutes later there was a knock on our door. There stood the frazzled Mrs. Slotnick. "Alright already, alright already, I'm sorry. Let the kinder, be kinder." (Let the children, be children).

* * *

Now let's get back to 1963; anyone in the hotel who knew Bella, could never imagine her losing her cool ... she was always sweet and calm. She would have loved to be able to interact more personally with the guests, but given her job responsibilities, she settled on deriving pleasure from her brief conversations with them on the switchboard. To supplement this, she was a notorious eavesdropper. Bella was a romantic and kept her eyes and ears open, to aid her in following the live soap opera existence of all the young attractive guests that occasionally resided at the hotel.

A punctual person, Mom always went to lunch promptly at noon and returned to her switchboard at 1 P.M. One Thursday, within minutes of her return, I received a frantic call, "**Herby, you have to do something! Anne Williams just committed suicide!**"

"Mom, how do you know?"

"Herby, I heard her."

"You heard her what?"

"I heard her tell someone."

"Mom, how could she have committed suicide, if she's still talking?"

"I don't know about that, but I think you better run up and find out."

Without any delay, I called Lincoln at the bell station and we both headed for the staircase. Climbing two and three steps at a time, we were at room 208 almost before Bella pulled the plug on our phone conversation. I knocked on the door. We received no reply. I opened the latch with my passkey and we cautiously entered the room.

The room was dimly lit. The only light came from the rays that filtered through the closed blinds. On the nightstand stood a bottle of Bourbon and what looked a prescription vial.

"Lincoln, throw on the lights!" I yelled.

I could now see that both the Bourbon and the vial were empty. On the double bed laid the sprawled out body of the extremely attractive Miss. Williams. She was lying on her back with one arm hanging over the side of the bed. Her eyes had a vacant look as though she was staring at the ceiling, her blond tresses flowed across her pillow and her opened, lacy negligee displayed her ample bosom and shapely figure. She was a sight to behold. I felt very uncomfortable because I found myself fighting the urge to look at her breasts.

Then I suddenly exclaimed, "**She's alive**!"

"How do you know?"

"Lincoln—look at her chest."

She was alive but her breathing was very shallow. We sprang into action—I grabbed one arm, Lincoln grabbed the other; we maneuvered her to the end of the bed and eased her into a sitting position. She was not responsive. I slapped her face a few times (I had seen this done in the movies) and she emitted a murmur. After a few more slaps Lincoln and I, with a forceful pull, stood her up. We proceeded to drag her about the room, not withstanding her wobbly legs. As we neared the phone

I propped her up against Lincoln, quickly picked up the phone and told Bella to call for an ambulance. We continued to drag her around, with occasional slaps, until the paramedics relieved us.

I never found out the reason for her attempted suicide and we never saw her again. Miss. Williams never knew that she owed her life to the romantic switchboard operator who lived vicariously through eavesdropping. Thursday, November 21, 1963, was the date that my mom also became half-a-doctor. The first life she saved was the life of Miss. Ann Williams from room 208.

This episode prompted me to be better prepared for future hotel disasters. I purchased two oxygen tanks and stored them at the front desk. I also posted suicide help telephone numbers at the switchboard and at the front desk. Hopefully, these efforts would save the life of any future suicidal guests.

* * *

The next day, at about 1:40 P.M, Mom ran frantically into my office, "Herby put on the television fast, something terrible has happened!" I quickly switched on Channel 2 just as Walter Cronkite, the CBS news anchorman, was interrupting *As the World Turns* with an announcement stating that President Kennedy had been seriously wounded in a shooting in downtown Dallas. At 2:37 P.M., a tearful Cronkite appeared live and read field reports indicating that our President had died.

Guests that were upstairs suddenly came down to the lobby crying. I walked out of the hotel and just started walking around aimlessly. Madison Avenue was starting to fill up with pedestrians. People were sobbing everywhere but there was no evidence of panic. On East 32nd Street, I happened upon one of our hotel guests, Sarah Fields. She had just gotten off the subway and was returning to the hotel after a shopping trip uptown.

She said in a tearful voice, "Mr. Sokol, you cannot believe what's doing down there! Everyone, I mean everyone, was crying in the subway car."

We walked back to the hotel together and found the lobby filled with concerned guests questioning each other for more information. They all seemed to be in a state of shock and feared that this might be the beginning of more ominous things to come. For the next four days, it was as if the country had shut down. The tragic assassination of our young, respected world leader, President John Fitzgerald Kennedy, put my insignificant travails into a more realistic perspective.

DIVERSIFICATION

In 1963 business was off considerably, at least with my investment group's properties. All of our buildings were either rooming houses or single room occupancy hotels. Some of these locations had coffee shops or restaurants with liquor, but all of the food operations were leased to restaurateurs. Since the hotel business was very weak, the partners, utilizing their unique naiveté, made a strategic decision to purchase a restaurant/cocktail lounge. I was impressed and excited. The location they chose was on East 37th Street right off Park Avenue. This was an upscale location with a lot of potential. The restaurant was in a thriving hotel and owned by a renowned developer who obviously did not want the hassle of restaurant management.

The first time I visited the property I was in awe. Upon entering the restaurant, I sank into thick, plush, red and gold carpeting. The upholstered chairs were a red and gold patterned cut velvet that matched the carpeting beautifully. I stood there gazing at the magnificent brass fixtures—the mahogany bar seemed to go on forever. I couldn't believe I was involved in this venture, even if it was as a small minority participant.

It did not take too long before my elation dissipated. The first month we ran the business to the tune of an $8,000 loss. The next month was not much better. An emergency meeting of the partners was called. A determination was made that our French speaking Maitre D' was responsible for the losses; the implication being that he had his hand in the till.

So in their infinite wisdom, the partners decided that my father-in-law, Hymie, should replace the Frenchman. The leasehold on the Sherman Square Hotel, that my father-in-law had been managing, had recently been sold. Therefore, my father-in-law was now available to take on a new position. More importantly, perhaps, was the fact that he had a very French looking, pencil moustache. If one didn't notice his prominent nose and his Yiddish accent, he could easily be taken for a Frenchman. As the new Maitre D' Hymie assumed the alias ... Pierre.

Bringing all his expertise from the butcher shop, photography studio and the recent hotel, Pierre miraculously pared $2,000 off the next month's losses. Now we were only losing $6,000 a month. Another emergency meeting was called. It was obvious that we could not last too much longer while hemorrhaging money at this pace. With the original French Maitre D' gone and operations of the restaurant in the capable hands of Pierre, they concluded that the losses must have been emanating from the liquor side of the operation. This was astounding to me because of the high margins yielded by the liquor as opposed to the food.

The partners tossed around various ideas concerning how they could bring trusted expertise to the business. They decided to take the following strategic initiative;

someone had to go to school and learn about beverage control. It wasn't too taxing to figure out who would become the student.

"Let's send Herby. He is a college graduate and would be capable of taking a beverage control course in a community college," suggested one partner.

"Good idea, he should be able to absorb the knowledge and apply it to our needs," added another.

They all agreed. So now the half-a-doctor went off to pursue his graduate degree in a community college of all places and in beverage control of all subjects. If you had told me five years ago that I would be studying beverage control, I would have thought you were crazy. But let's face it; now that I was a hotel manager, I had plenty of time on my hands. In-between fixing toilets and refrigerators, doing the payroll, running the asylum, trying to abort suicides and defending myself against violent armed and unarmed attackers, I could certainly squeeze in time to enhance my education. The one good thing about "Bronx Community College" was that it was a quick subway ride from home.

* * *

Both Annette and I were really Brooklynites. When we got married in 1958, it was extremely difficult to find an available rent-controlled apartment. Annette's Uncle Sol was able to secure a spacious, three-room apartment overlooking the reservoir for us, and the rent was only $78 per month. The problem was ... it was in the Bronx. We moved there for financial reasons and felt as though we had gone into exile. We were too far from lifelong friends, most of our relatives, and all social interaction.

I am not sure about Annette, but I felt (and hoped) that we were there on a temporary basis. Not only did I shy away from initiating new friendships, I also refused to learn the street names in our neighborhood, except for Sedgwick Avenue (the one on which we resided).

* * *

Now, let's get back to school. The course work in Beverage Control was basically common sense. Part of the class work introduced equipment that would facilitate portioning out drinks. The area that I was most interested in, of course, was identifying underhanded activities by bartenders. After three months I graduated with honors; I was anxious to go to the lounge and apply my professional skills. By the time I finished the course, profits were still non-existent, and the business was at its death knell. It was imperative that I apply my knowledge quickly and efficiently.

Now, forty-seven years later, I can still remember walking into the lounge area of the restaurant. It was 5:20 P.M. The bar was dimly lit and packed with *the beautiful people*—corporate executives, their mistresses, their girlfriends, singles, etc. They were packed five deep at the bar. Since none of the employees knew me except for Pierre, I didn't have to worry about being recognized. I was just another customer.

This place has to be a gold mine, I thought to myself. The losses puzzled me! I sat down at a corner table with good visibility of the bar and the bartenders. I ordered a Manhattan, a popular drink at that time. As I nursed the drink, I stared intently at the two bartenders. They were fast, efficient and friendly. My community college trained eyes observed nothing out of order. There was no spillage, no overly generous drinks, no free drinks, and certainly no pocketing of any money.

Should I order another drink? Why not? I ordered another Manhattan and continued to observe. I started to feel that this exercise was a waste of time. If one of the bartenders were involved in under-handed activities, he certainly would have taken advantage of a busy evening such as this. In addition to watching the bartenders, I also did a little people watching. It was hard not to notice the attractive women. As I sipped my Manhattan, I noticed a well-dressed gentleman, sporting a power tie, approach the corner of the bar.

I heard him quietly say, "I'll have the usual, Tim."

Tim turned, picked up the phone and said something that I couldn't hear. (Later I found out that was how he communicated with the wine steward.) In next to no time, a bus boy appeared carrying a case of Canadian Club and handed it to the well-dressed gentleman. The man turned, nodded to Tim and proceeded to walk out with the case.

My God! I couldn't believe my eyes. We're not losing money by the drink. **IT'S BY THE CASE**! I was in total shock—but the mystery was solved. Unfortunately, even though the operation was successful, the patient died. By the time I figured out how we were losing money, we were practically in bankruptcy. Instead of going to Community College, I should have just sat in the bar three months earlier and observed a few typical nights. I think I could have figured out the cause of the problem without my new graduate degree. By the time I solved the mystery, the partners were already frantically seeking a purchaser for the restaurant/lounge carcass. Ironically, an hour after we closed on the sale, the Marshall appeared to place a padlock on the front door. We considered ourselves very lucky that day.

* * *

At the same time that Pierre was managing the restaurant, our partnership group was also running a somewhat upscale hotel. This hotel was in the East 40's off Lexington Avenue. It was an excellent location because of the nearby presence of the United Nations and many corporate headquarters. The hotel was being actively managed by one of the partners who had been an Israeli Air Force pilot in his younger years. Unfortunately for all concerned this property was also not too profitable.

Occupying the street level of the hotel was an upscale restaurant and lounge that was leased to a different management group. They appeared to be deriving exceptional financial gains from the restaurant/lounge. I don't recall who it was that precipitated what happened next but the bottom line was that our illustrious partners exchanged the hotel lease for the thriving restaurant. All the partners were jubilant. The profits exceeded our best expectations.

It didn't take long for the smiles to leave their faces. Suddenly, the profits dropped precipitously. At the same time the hotel started to run ninety percent occupancy. We would have loved to discover what the hotel management did to increase their profits. We did, soon, discover what our restaurant management did to decrease our profits.

The restaurant/lounge was, as I said, an upscale location and, therefore, required the services of a hatcheck girl. (Yes, men's hats were in fashion during those years.) The hatcheck girl was an extremely attractive, efficient, young, bosomy woman and she dressed to accent her best assets. Our courageous ex-pilot had taken his eyes off the ball and focused them upon the bosom of our fair maiden at the expense of the restaurant business. The ex-pilot was given strong warnings from the investment group as well as his wife. They all agreed that if this man was ever caught fooling around again, he would be thrown out!

Again, it was too late—the restaurant corporation filed for bankruptcy shortly after. I was beginning to see a trend here. (Years later, by the way, that hotel lease was sold for millions.) I was the young kid on the block—all the other partners were about twenty-five years older than I was, and most had many years of experience in hotel operations and management. One was actually a Certified Public Accountant. However, I was beginning to wonder if they really knew what they were doing.

New York World's Fair - 1964 to 1965

O ur diversification effort was over and the hotel business was at its lowest ebb, the only thing we had going for us was the anticipation of the 1964 "New York World's Fair". Business had dropped to the point where I would have to go to the bank every day, to deposit our daily proceeds, thereby ensuring that we could make that week's payroll.

The "New York World's Fair" was the concept of a group of businessmen, who firmly believed that it would create a financial boom for New York City, by increasing the amount of tourism. To accomplish this, Robert Moses was recruited to head their newly formed corporation. Robert Moses was a logical choice because he had served as Parks Commissioner for decades and was responsible for successfully building much of the New York City park system. The fair was to run for two years with two six-month seasons from April to October.

The 1964/1965 "World's Fair" was developed and took place without being sanctioned by the *Bureau of International Expositions* because no one country is allowed to hold more than one fair within a ten-year period. Given that the "Seattle World's Fair" had been sanctioned as the host in 1962, New York was not able to receive approval from the *B.I.E.* I didn't believe sanctioning would be a make or break factor for our hotel, but according to the official records, the fair was almost a disaster. The "New York World's Fair" lost possible participants such as Canada, Australia, the Soviet Union and most of the European nations. I was led to believe that the corporation running the fair almost declared bankruptcy before the second season began. However, it did manage to hang on.

The finances of the "New York World's Fair" were really insignificant to me. What was important were the millions of individuals and families expected to visit New York. There was no way that we would not get a tremendous shot in the arm from it. My gamble was to minimize long stay check-ins and keep rooms available for the anticipated onslaught to arrive.

The Roger Williams Hotel never needed a reservation system before and I believed that such procedures had to be put in place. To that end, I purchased a chart board that enabled me to post and review the expected reservations. I also visited the large transient hotels to try and convince the managers that our hotel could and would effectively handle their overflow.

We had a lot of work before us. The hotel had to be spruced up and put into good order. If complaints would surface the first season, the second would surely be a disaster. I must say I was extremely proud of my staff's effort and dedication to accomplish our goals.

The first season began with the anticipated results. We were filled with transients, mostly families that realized that our kitchenettes would save them considerable expenses during their stay. I tried as best I could, to keep our *inmates* under control, so as to avoid embarrassment. However, I hadn't anticipated the arrival of *new transient weirdoes*.

COITUS NON-INTERUPTUS - ROOM 604

It was the spring of 1964, the start of the first "New York World's Fair" season, and also the start of the air-conditioning installation season. All of our accommodations were equipped with window air-conditioners that Ernie and I installed every spring and then removed every fall. We would place four to six units on a flatbed hand truck, take the service elevator to the floor we were working on, and go down the hallway installing the units, one by one, into the room windows. It was a tiresome and difficult chore, but one that had to be done. After completing the job in one room, I would use the service elevator phone to call the desk and find out if the next one was occupied and if so by whom. (There was no such thing as a cell phone then.)

One day after we had finished putting the unit into room 603, I called to find out if 604 was occupied. I was informed that it was ... by a tourist visiting the fair. I knocked on the door of 604.

A male voice screamed out, "Who is it?"

"It's Mr. Sokol, the manager, and my engineer. We're here to install your window air conditioner."

"Great! Come right in; it's getting stuffy in here," he answered in a loud voice.

We waited for him to open the door. After a few moments, I realized that I might as well use the passkey; he didn't seem to be coming to the door. The lights were off, and it would take a few moments for my eyes to acclimate to the dimness. As we pushed the cart past the foyer, I heard sounds from the bedroom area. We continued to approach the window, and suddenly—I saw two naked bodies, on the bed, copulating with extreme vigor!

"Oops, I'm terribly sorry," I uttered embarrassedly.

"It's okay, come on in," the heaving body replied as he waved us in.

Ernie was hesitant and whispered to me, "Let's get out of here, Boss."

But I pushed him forward; I figured if it's all right with the copulators, it's all right with me. I must say that the distraction did not deter us—we installed the unit in record time while listening to the sounds of the thrusts and moans. As a matter of fact we finished before he did! On our way out, this character actually waved good-bye to us. Unfortunately for Ernie, the only one receiving a tip was the young woman.

BAREFOOT IN THE LOBBY - ROOM 1002

On another day during that first Fair season, I once again had to fill in for the 4 P.M. to midnight shift. It was about 9 P.M. and all the expected new arrivals had been checked in. The lobby was empty and I decided it was time to sit down and relax at the front desk for a while. I poured myself a cup of hot coffee, added a spoonful of sugar, and as I stirred, I walked to the high stool at the desk. Just as soon as I sat down—I jumped up again. The self-service elevator doors had opened and walking straight toward me was Mrs. Edwards. She was a "New York World's Fair" visitor from Dayton, Ohio and the occupant of room 1002. This woman was a shapely, fairly attractive, blond woman about forty to forty-five years of age. As she continued to approach me, I stood there dumbfounded with my mouth agape. **Mrs. Edwards was absolutely, one hundred percent nude!** She was wearing nothing but a ridiculous grin. Looking at her from my frontal view advantage, it was very apparent that the hair on her head did not use the contents of a bottle from the beauty salon. Mrs. Edwards walked up to the front desk and placed her left elbow upon it. She then rested her chin on her hand. Her derriere was positioned so that it pointed to the glass doors of the front lobby.

I gasped and blurted out, "Ma'am, you are naked!"

This was an obvious observation, but in my stupefied state, I truly was at a loss for words.

Smiling, she calmly asked, "Are there any messages for me?"

"No ma'am. Listen, I'm afraid you'll get pneumonia running around like that; let me get you a blanket."

I was fearful that a normal guest might enter and wonder what kind of establishment they were vacationing in. Fortunately, because of all the new transient arrivals we kept extra blankets at the desk. I quickly grabbed one and threw it around her shoulders. At the same time, I spun her around and pointed her directly toward the elevator. I pushed the button, and as soon as the elevator doors opened, I gently shoved her in. She ascended, just as the couple that were guests in 1209, walked through our entrance doors. As they waited for the elevator to arrive, I prayed that my naked guest wouldn't still be riding in it. When the doors opened, I fearfully closed my eyes. I heard no shriek, and thus assumed it was safe to take a peek. The couple entered the elevator car without any disastrous scene. Looking at the elevator indicator, I watched in anticipation and breathed a sigh of relief, when it stopped on twelve without a detour. Still transfixed on the dial, *I breathed in deeply*, because I saw that the car had stopped on the tenth floor again on the way down. A few moments later the doors reopened, and sure enough out strutted Mrs. Edwards, still totally naked and dragging the blanket behind her. She looked like a toddler dragging a security blanket, but the toddler probably would have some clothes on. Again I spun her around, shoved her back into the elevator and punched the tenth floor button. As the car ascended I thought to myself, should I call Bellevue ... the police ... or maybe recruiters for a strip joint? She certainly had the appropriate assets.

Before I could even dial a number, the elevator returned with my naked guest ... sans blanket. Leaving my post at the front desk, I forced her back into the elevator and accompanied her to the tenth floor. I personally escorted her to her room, opened her door and pushed her in.

Emphatically, I said, "**Look, this shit has got to stop!** Why don't you just lie down and sleep it off! Good night!"

During my entire shift my stomach lurched each time the elevator door opened, but I guess she took my advice because I didn't see her again that night. The rest of my evening shift was calm and relaxing. Couples and families were returning from their day at the "World's Fair". These normal people brought me back to Planet Earth with their exuberance. Many shared their day's experiences with me. I made a mental note to take my family to the "World's Fair" soon.

My Neighbor's Indiscretion - Room 207

A third incident that remains indelibly etched in my memory occurred during one of the New York City sellout days. It was about noontime, when the desk clerk from the Commodore Hotel called, asked if we had any space available, and if so could we accommodate a referral.

"We'd be happy to help," I answered.

"Mr. Richard Sonsky will be over in fifteen minutes; please have a double room ready for him."

I walked over to the front desk, jotted down the name and alerted my desk clerk about the anticipated new arrival. Then I proceeded to the coffee shop to pick up the hot pastrami on rye and black coffee that I had previously ordered. Upon returning to the lobby, I began to reflect on the name Mr. Richard Sonsky. I thought could it be ... nah ... it probably wasn't.

As I opened the door to the front desk area, the lobby entrance doors opened as well and in walked *the couple*. I startled the day clerk as I suddenly dove to the floor and splattered my coffee onto his trousers. As I huddled against the front partition, I put my fingers to my mouth and shook my head signaling silence. He was bewildered but did his best to ignore me and check in our new guests. They registered as Mr. and Mrs. Sonsky. It seemed like an eternity, as I lay on the floor and waited for the bellman to escort our new check-ins to the elevator.

Once they were out of sight, the clerk motioned to me that it was safe to rejoin the world. The reason for my dramatic action was because Mr. and Mrs. Sonsky were members of my temple; but that wasn't Mrs. Sonsky. I had this very confused reaction ... I didn't know if **I** felt embarrassed or if I felt embarrassed for **him**. The real Mrs. Sonsky was a lovely, attractive, personable woman and the mother of one of my daughter's good friends. The imposter looked like someone that he had dragged out of a sewer. Why would any man do this? Reflecting back upon that day, I wonder how he would have reacted if I had been the person that greeted him at the desk.

IS IT HARD TO CHANGE A BULB? - ROOM 708

During the fair, we had countless incidents that were extremely funny and sadly, quite a few tragedies as well. At the time, the following occurrence almost traumatized me. Nowadays, when I think about this event, I think it is hysterically funny. An elderly woman (you know, someone about my present age) had checked in from Florida. I think she had come up to see her family and take in the Fair as well.

It was 5:30 PM when Mrs. Solomon, the guest in room 708, called down that she required assistance. I dispatched Earl, who was at the bell stand that evening, to find out what the problem was. Upon his return, he reported that the bulb in the ceiling fixture had burned out and needed replacement. Since the engineer and the handyman had left for the day, I grabbed a few bulbs and went up to take care of the problem myself.

I guess I didn't think it through completely. When I got to the room, I realized that there was no way that I, a height-challenged person, could reach the fixture without a ladder. Not wanting to waste time by securing one, I asked Mrs. Solomon to please stand aside while I carried an end table to the center of the room. Then I

155

placed a straight back kitchen chair onto the table and proceeded to climb onto the table and then onto the chair. As I reached up to replace the bulb, so did Mrs. Solomon ... but not to change a bulb.

Just try to picture this scene: I am precariously perched on a chair, which is balanced on a table, my hands are stretched upward, and she is assaulting my genitalia and smiling from ear to ear to boot. She wasn't letting go. I thought to myself this couldn't possibly be happening.

As I screamed, "**Let go of my balls!** " I started to wobble and the chair and I fell over.

Thank God she let go as I was falling or Annette would have been pretty upset. I was more irate than bruised and I started to lambaste her with every profanity I could muster up. My blood pressure must have hit new heights ... she just stood there with an innocent smirk.

My departing words were, "Good day, madam, you will just have to survive without this light," and I escaped as quickly as possible.

When I returned to the lobby the desk clerk asked, "Why are you so flustered?"

I simply answered, "When you have an opportunity, try to convince Mrs. Solomon to become a permanent guest. She would fit perfectly in our asylum."

The "New York World's Fair" ended in October 1965, and I am happy to report that we had successfully replenished our coffers. We now had grandiose plans to update and refurnish the hotel. Even the occasional asylum incidents could not dampen my spirits. Everything was moving in a positive direction.

FUN IN THE DARK

After the "World's Fair", my spirits were really flying high. Though I still had a lot to learn, I was confident in my ability to take this business to the next level. I could not imagine anything that could interfere with our operation. This smugness was quickly dispelled.

It was November 9, 1965, 5 P.M. My mom was finished with her day's work; she said good-bye and left. The subway station was a few blocks away and from there she would take the train home to Brooklyn. I, on the other hand, was settling in for another unexpected, and unwanted, evening shift. I called the nearby deli and ordered a corned beef on seeded rye, with lots of mustard, and a coke for dinner. Then I sat down at the front desk and picked up the *New York Post*. After reading the evening newspaper for a few, wonderful, peaceful minutes, I looked at my watch for no particular reason, and noted that that it was 5:26 P.M. I guess I was curious to see how long I could sit and relax.

Suddenly, a minute later, the lights went out! As I stood up to call Ernie and get him to fix the electrical problem, I glanced outside and noticed that we were not alone in the darkness. It wasn't long before I learned that the entire northeast area of the United States and large parts of Canada had gone dark. From Buffalo to the eastern border of New Hampshire and from New York City to Ontario, a massive power outage had struck without warning. Trains were stuck between subway stops, and people were trapped in elevators. It was approximated that ten thousand commuters were stuck on subway cars. After Ernie and I safely extricated our three, grateful guests from the hotel's self-service elevator, I decided to take a walk outside to see what was happening.

Our traffic signals had failed and traffic was brought to a standstill. The roads were in complete darkness except for the headlights of the struggling vehicles. It looked as though New York City was in total chaos. But despite this, commuters, pedestrians, and on-lookers all seemed to be handling the stress well. Strangers were helping strangers. Drivers were offering rides to stranded pedestrians. It gave me a warm feeling to see New Yorkers extending outstretched hands to people they didn't even know.

The hotel was located in the center of the lingerie, furniture, and carpet business centers. Their respective office employees, ready for the commute home were forced to find lodging. Some of them slept in their offices overnight, some hung out in Penn Station and/ or Grand Central Station, and many others called The Roger Williams Hotel.

Luckily, our switchboard was operating because AT&T had its own generators. The phone was ringing off the hook with requests for lodging for the night. I only had twenty rooms available, and they were dispersed throughout our sixteen floors.

My next dilemma involved getting our rush of new guests to their rooms without elevators and without lights. I ran around the corner to the neighborhood grocery store and purchased all the candles they had in stock, along with matches. First, I used a few candles to light the lobby and the front desk, which actually created a party-like atmosphere in the lobby. But now—how was I going to get the guests to their rooms? Unfortunately, I only had a limited number of candles. I came up with a mathematical solution. When a guest checked in and I assigned room 207, for example, I would do a quick calculation, take out a knife, and chop two inches off the candle. I figured one inch per floor. I needed one candle for the guest and one to allow our bellman to return. After a while the bellman was so exhausted from his trips up and down the steps, that I just gave the appropriate inches of candle to the guest and prayed that he or she would find their way on their own. If I miscalculated, they just might have to sleep on the staircase or in a hallway ... at least they would be warm.

In a relatively short period of time, the lobby was packed. It was wall-to-wall people. Some were guests and some were just walk-ins looking to commiserate with anyone who would listen to their plight. To prevent the lobby from bursting from the sheer mass of humanity within it, I opened the lobby door to the coffee shop (which always closed after lunch). The coffee shop looked very romantic with the lit candles that I placed on the tables, and some of our *lobby guests* moved in there. I broke open some bottles of wine that I had sequestered in my office and offered it to those in the lobby—I kept the Dewars for myself. It was now truly beginning to resemble a gala party.

Around 6:30 P.M. the front doors opened and in walked **my mother**. I was so thrilled to see that she had come back to the hotel and was not stuck on a subway train somewhere. I took my mother into my office and told her that I would give her a room on the second floor, so she could go to sleep for the night.

She smiled at me and replied, "Why would I want to be alone in a room when I could be down here with people?"

Mom thought this was the greatest—a social gathering right here in our hotel, finally, an opportunity to talk to people, in person, without earphones on her head. I saved the room for her anyway. I figured that by midnight she would need some sleep.

By 11 P.M. the power was restored to 75% of Brooklyn and by 2 A.M. that borough was completely restored with electricity. By midnight much of the Bronx and Queens were illuminated and by 7 A.M., almost fourteen hours after the blackout began, our entire city was restored with power.

It was one of the most exciting nights that I have ever experienced. I didn't close my eyes for one minute during the entire night. It has been written that many babies were conceived that evening. I am sure that our hotel contributed our fair share to the number.

This unanticipated event reinforced my belief in the good character of people, and the camaraderie and subsequent ability of people, including myself, to cope during a major emergency situation.

THE INVADERS - ROOM 1011

Occupying room 1011 was a monthly tenant by the name of John Connor. He was a short man, with passable looks, short brown hair and small, light brown eyes. Mr. Connor was a retired, middle-level manager who enjoyed taking a nip or two each day. Since his retirement, though, he started to increase his daily intake of alcohol and could now, I believed, be considered an alcoholic. As far as we knew he had no family, or at least none that cared enough to call or visit him. He probably had lost contact with any business acquaintances, and definitely had no friends that he kept in touch with. However, as far as I was concerned, he was the ideal tenant. He paid his rent on time and never created any disturbances or difficulties for staff members or other guests. That is until the day when a frantic call came down from room 1010. The transient guest stated that no sooner had she entered her room, than she heard piercing screams emanating from the adjacent room.

Mom connected me to room 1010 and after our guest reiterated her frantic statement, I said, "Tell me exactly what you are hearing."

To which she replied, "It sounds like a man is being tortured." I thanked her for alerting us and assured her that we would send security up immediately.

An uncomfortable feeling was growing inside of me. What if an intruder was assaulting him? Now I never was and still am not the hero type. However, as I previously indicated, I preferred to solve problems, *in-house*, if possible. So I called Ernie and told him I needed his help and possibly his muscle. Ernie joined me in the lobby and the two of us, using the service elevator, ascended to the tenth floor. We were able to hear Connor's frightened screams the minute the elevator reached the floor.

I knocked on his door, and we were greeted with screams of, "**HELP! HELP!**"

I used my passkey to gain entry and found a petrified, shaking Mr. Connor cowering in the far corner of his room.

"Mr. Connor, what's wrong?" I asked, trying to stay calm.

"**Look—look, there—don't you see them? Little, purple people, they're everywhere. They're trying to kill me, they're trying to kill me!**"

Ernie and I glanced around and, of course, saw absolutely nothing unusual.

He fell backward, his feet started thrashing mid-air and while pulling at his throat screamed, "**Help me! This one is choking me!**"

It was obvious that he was delusional. Either he was experiencing delirium tremors or his mind had entirely snapped. Either way, I decided that we had to do whatever we could to help calm him down. I walked to his side and feigned grabbing the little, purple person from his throat. I struggled with him and threw a few punches at this little devil.

"Take that, POW, BAM," I yelled. Images of an episode of Batman, my kids had watched the prior day, quickly fleeting through my mind. I screamed to Ernie, **"Open the window!"**

He promptly did as I asked. I then proceeded to throw the invader ten stories to his demise. Ernie got into the fray, and he started punching and throwing the succumbed little, purple people out the window along with me. It was a difficult fight for we were gravely outnumbered but after a few more minutes of this deadly battle, we managed to subdue all the invaders and escape unscathed.

"Do you see any more?" I inquired of Mr. Connor.

His bulging, fearful eyes searched the small room until he warily agreed that we had gotten rid of all of them. We helped him get up from the floor and sat him in an armchair. Ernie gave him a glass of water and we patiently reassured him that we would always be there for him, if he should ever need our help again. We left exhausted but with a sense of pride ... knowing that we had just restored peace and order to a kind man, who resided in the strange and chaotic world of room 1011, or the further removed world of his imagination. The two of us then returned downstairs to continue our *normal* activities.

THE PHILANDERING DOCTOR - ROOM 1204

After marrying and moving to the Bronx, I lost contact with my Brooklyn brethren. I knew this was not unusual because interests and priorities change, and friends simply drift apart. However, I really missed the pals from my youth and I wanted to reestablish contact. Therefore, one day, I called three of my closest friends and asked if they would like to get together and see a Knick game in Madison Square Garden the following Sunday. All three responded positively. It was February of 1966, and I hadn't spoken to any of them since I was a pharmacist over five years ago. I informed them of my new vocation and suggested we meet at The Roger Williams Hotel at 6:30 P.M.; I looked forward to showing them around my new working environment. They all agreed and the date was set.

I walked out the entrance doors at 6:20 P.M. anxiously awaiting the arrival of my long-lost friends. It was a cold, winter evening. The wind was blowing through my hair, and the snow was still piled along the curbs from yesterday's six-inch snowfall. It was sad to see how the beautiful white snow of yesterday had turned gray and black from the city's pollution and endless traffic.

My friends arrived at the hotel promptly and I proudly ushered them into our tiny lobby. I took them up to view a few of our newly decorated rooms and expounded on my responsibilities and daily chores. They were quite impressed. On the surface, an outsider looking in could wrongly assume this was a fairly modern, successful, transient hotel.

While descending, in the elevator, I brought them up to date on my family ... Annette and I were now the proud parents of three children. Sharyn had just celebrated her sixth birthday, our daughter Jodi was three and our baby, David, was ten months old.

When we returned to the lobby, I pointed out the beautiful French phone that I had personally installed onto a marble column. This was my contribution to the lobby modernization program. My friends didn't seem too impressed with it.

At this point, I figured it was time to leave, "Why don't we head out to the Garden," I suggested.

As we were walking toward the doors, all of us momentarily stopped and gaped at the stunning, thirty-five to forty year old, stately and elegantly dressed woman who had just entered. She was wearing a luxurious, dark brown mink coat and stylish high-heeled brown suede boots. After glancing around the lobby, she approached my French phone. Since I didn't recognize her, and being naturally curious, I motioned to my friends to wait a moment. The attractive woman picked up the phone and calmly asked the operator to connect her with Mrs.

Staley. I was familiar with Mrs. Staley, so my curiosity level was raised even more.

Immediately after hearing a response, the attractive woman's face took on a contorted expression and suddenly she started to scream, "I know who you are; I found out all about you—you slut; you're sleeping with my husband; you better get your ass down here right away! I'm in the lobby!"

Game time or no game time, you can be sure my friends were not leaving now. They couldn't wait to see Mrs. Staley. Their imaginations must have been going wild. Recalling that the guest was the monthly tenant that occupied room 1204, I looked up at the elevator indicator and noticed that it had reached the twelfth floor. As it started its descent, I scratched my head in bewilderment. This had to be a mistake, I thought.

The elevator doors opened and the scene that enfolded before us was as if we were thrust into the midst of a "Twilight Zone" episode. Mrs. Staley, a woman in her late 70's, walked slowly out of the elevator. She was physically feeble, had gray matted hair, a heavily wrinkled face, a very pale pallor, and was missing a few front teeth. She could easily have passed for one of Macbeth's witches. As she entered the lobby the visitor started screaming, "You are fucking my husband, I would like to strangle you ... you disgusting whore. I despise you!"

The looks on my friends' faces were priceless. Here was this absolutely gorgeous lady accusing an elderly, repulsive, looking woman of adultery. The betrayed wife, in her deranged state, must have envisioned Marilyn Monroe standing there. The only thing that I could figure was that the accuser was so filled with rage and fury that she did not see what her assumed adversary looked like.

I immediately walked over to Mrs. Staley, took her arm, escorted her back to the elevator and apologized for the rudeness of the unknown woman. After seeing that the elevator was ascending, I turned my attention back to the stranger.

To her I sternly said, "Madam, I am the General Manager of this hotel and I am asking you to leave immediately or I will call the police. It is shameful that you spoke to Mrs. Staley in that manner."

She started to say something ... thought twice about it, turned and quickly left.

The next day I got the scoop on the actual story. I spoke with Mrs. Staley, who had almost calmed down from the incident of the previous day. I learned that the attractive wife resided in Philadelphia, and was married to a successful physician. The good doctor was a kind and generous man, who had taken it upon himself to help out a dear, elderly friend of his deceased parents. He was intent on helping her live out her remaining years in comfort. He did this by occasionally visiting Mrs. Staley and by sending her generous checks to help support her. It was the discovery of these checks that flipped out the doctor's wife.

SCRATCH ME, SCRATCH ME - ROOM 1018

It was a Sunday in June when Stuart Braverman stopped by to inquire about our accommodations and rate structure. He introduced himself and enthusiastically explained that he was about to embark on an exciting career in radio. He was a recent graduate of New York University with a degree in communications. Stuart was a nice looking, young man standing about 6' tall with a lean, athletic looking 175-pound build. He was clean-shaven and sported a healthy head of brown wavy hair. Despite his prominent nose, some would consider him handsome.

The enthusiasm he exuded about his future profession was refreshing, "Of course, I'll only be a gofer in the beginning, but the station manager assured me that my career path will be an accelerated one."

Stuart said he would require a decent sized room with bath and cooking facilities and would appreciate a weekly rate. He mentioned that during his years at college he lived at the N.Y.U. dorms, which were not too far from the hotel. His family resided in Rye, New York, a suburb in Westchester. Determined to be independent, Stuart wanted to rent a room of his own and looked forward to beginning his new lifestyle. Since his budget was limited, I had Lincoln show him room 1018. It was a relatively small room, facing the rear, but equipped with private bath, kitchenette, television and air conditioning. Upon returning, he secured the room with a deposit and indicated that he would be checking in on Monday.

He turned out to be a good guest with absolutely no demands. You now know all that I knew or would ever get to know about Stuart Braverman's past, or his new job. About one month later, there were some changes in his appearance. Facial tics developed, and he seemed to be uncomfortable in his well-tailored suits. Intermittently, he would shrug his shoulders as if he was trying to dislodge something beneath his jacket. Then one day, about six weeks into his stay, Stuart stopped at the desk and asked to see me. Tom was on duty; he called me and explained the situation. I gave him the okay and then Tom showed him into my office. I motioned to Stuart to sit down, but he seemed uncomfortable and insisted upon standing.

"How can I help you, Stuart?"

"I have a problem—my back itches."

I honestly thought he was joking.

"Please, could you scratch my back?"

"Stuart, you are kidding, I hope."

"No, please ... I am beside myself. Could you please scratch my back?"

I stood up, turned him toward the door, and gently started scratching his back. He froze, and urged me to scratch some more. No one could see this spectacle, so I scratched him for a little while longer.

Five days past before I saw Stuart again. It was Friday evening and Stuart was coming into the hotel as I was leaving. He grabbed my arm and frantically said, "Please, please help me! Scratch me!" In view of the fact that we were standing in the lobby, I just gave him a quick scratch and rapidly turned and left to catch my express bus home.

* * *

I was looking forward to spending some time with my family. I was always off on Saturdays; it was the middle of summer, and the weather was fantastic. We had plans to see how the building of our new house was progressing. By the beginning of the school year we would be living in a four-bedroom, colonial home in Rockland County, South Spring Valley to be exact. After checking out the progress on our dream house, we planned to go to Sebago Beach. Annette and I enjoyed relaxing on the sand while the children were happy digging and building castles. David was now two years old and could sit and play with sand for quite awhile. To keep the children happy we alternated playtime in the sand, with playtime in the water.

* * *

Over the weekend, I dismissed Mr. Stuart Braverman and his itches from my thoughts. Monday evening, about 5 P.M., I was completing some bookkeeping chores in my office when Stuart once again appeared at the front desk. He told Tom that it was urgent; he had to speak with Mr. Sokol. Tom, being sensitive to Mr. Braverman's sense of urgency, ushered him into my office again. I looked up and saw Stuart standing there with an expression of hopelessness and despair. *For the third time, he pleaded with me to scratch his back.* As I scratched him, I tried to convince him that his problem exceeded the realm of my expertise. I suggested he visit a dermatologist. I also made a mental note to bring in a Chinese backscratcher for him. Eventually, with reluctance he left, and I proceeded to go home.

Stuart never got to a Dermatologist. He found a much quicker resolution for his itch. At 10:15 that very same evening, he leapt from his tenth floor window. I was extremely distraught to hear of the death of Stuart Braverman and the waste of this very promising, young life. It took me a long time to recover from the shock and from my feelings of guilt. I couldn't help thinking about what I could have possibly done to help him, other than just scratching his back. Many years later I thought to myself, I guess after three scratches you're out ... the window.

THE PIXIE WHO COULDN'T FLY - ROOM 1404

There I was ... batting .500. Not a bad average if you're playing baseball—a piss poor one for saving lives. Though the responsibility of saving lives was not in my job description I, nevertheless, felt it was incumbent upon me to do so. I was sincerely laden with guilt. Truly, Stuart did not demonstrate the emotions I would expect from a potential suicide victim. However, my thoughts kept returning to the last night I saw him. Could I have prevented him from taking such desperate actions? Deep down, I knew the answer. I believe Stuart was headed for self-destruction before we even met and so was Anne Williams, but fortunately with the help of Mom she was saved.

A year later my batting average would take another drop, and on this occasion, I think I could have been the savior. I don't know when she checked in, but I could not help noticing her leaving and returning to the hotel. Ms. Joan Kadash was about 30 years old, adorable and vivacious. Just 5' 2" tall with short pixyish hair, she resembled a much prettier Edith Piaf. Whenever I saw her I couldn't help but wonder what she did for a living. I dismissed "working girl" for she seemed too sweet and besides that she never had any visitors. I somehow didn't think she was a corporate business employee either; she just didn't have that corporate look. Because of her early departures, I ruled out show business. Even Mom couldn't give me any input since Ms. Kadash received no calls. After awhile, I stopped playing the guessing game and turned my thoughts to more important matters—until that fateful day.

* * *

My long hours at the hotel precluded me from any organized sports activities, and random golf was for rich people; that left bowling, an activity one could participate in when time was available. Annette and I had made arrangements to meet my sister, Carol and her husband, Buddy, at the Whitestone Bowling Lanes at 8 P.M. on Sunday. That meant I would definitely have to leave the hotel by 5 P.M., at the latest, in order for us to have dinner and then drive to Whitestone.

I was right on schedule. At exactly five, I entered the lobby ready to start the trip. Ms. Kadash was sitting on the sofa and motioned me to join her. I didn't recall ever exchanging one word with her, but perhaps we might have a quick chat. That might help me resolve my curiosity about her. As I sat down on the chair opposite her, I introduced myself; I was sure she didn't know who I was. She smiled and said her name was Joan, and yes, she knew that I was the manager of the hotel. We spoke pleasantries for almost ten minutes, at which time I glanced at the clock hanging over the guest mailboxes and realized that I had to bring this conversation to an end.

"I am really happy that I had the opportunity to get to know you Joan, I am afraid I must be leaving now because I have a dinner appointment."

Suddenly, there was a look of panic on her face, and tears started to flow.

I continued, "I am terribly sorry, I didn't mean to upset you or be disrespectful, but I do have to go."

"Oh, please don't go." Joan pleaded. **"I need to talk."**

Okay, so I'll be a little late for bowling. She needs to cry it out. Perhaps she was just jilted by a boyfriend; even worse, maybe there was a death in the family. I have to admit my interest was somewhat piqued and so I remained. After a few random sentences, her words turned to gibberish. She spoke, but nothing intelligible passed her lips. As I started to rise, she again became coherent and pleaded with me to stay and talk. I remained seated and stared intently at her. Again her words became gibberish.

Realizing that aside from taking up space, I wasn't contributing anything to this conversation, I again said, "Look Joan, I really have to leave. Why don't I call you tomorrow and we can continue talking."

With that, I abruptly stood and left before her tears could dissuade me. I took the express bus to the Bronx and met Annette, who was visiting with her parents. Then we drove to Stella D'Oro, on Broadway in Riverdale, for a quick dinner. Annette just loved their stracciatella soup and anytime we were in the neighborhood, we had to go there so she could have their soup. We also had a few slices of pizza and soda. After our hurried dinner we continued to the Whitestone Lanes. With all our rushing, we were still fifteen minutes late. Carol and Buddy were anxiously awaiting our arrival.

In the middle of the first game, I heard my name being paged over the loud speaker. Well I don't know about you, but I had a pretty good idea why I was being paged. Sometime after Joan Kadash returned to her fourteenth floor room, she proceeded to remove all of her clothing and jump naked from her window, landing on Madison Avenue. On her descent, she narrowly missed a Japanese banker who was also a guest at the hotel.

Since I was the last person to be seen having contact with her, I was summoned from the bowling alley to return to the hotel. That was the end of bowling for Annette and me for that night. We got into the car and drove to the hotel. Fortunately, the identification process was done before my arrival—I really would have had trouble handling that. The police were waiting for me in Miss. Kadash's room. After speaking with them and trying to describe the last conversation I had with her, I was dismissed and returned to the lobby.

I just stood there staring at the sofa that Joan had sat on only a few hours ago. I couldn't help but think, would her life have been spared if I had spent another hour or two listening to her incoherent utterances or had her fate been previously sealed? Then I wondered if the hospital supply house would accept the return of two unused oxygen tanks? They don't seem to be doing anyone any good here.

CULTURAL DIFFERENCES

Since our accommodations had kitchenettes, we were able to entice United Nations representatives and their support personnel, as well as other types of executives from foreign countries who had unique dietary needs. We had many individuals from India, as well as Japan. We tried, as best we could, to keep guests from the same country on the same floor. Hence, there were times when exiting the elevator onto the eleventh floor that you would be overcome with the smell of curry. Similarly, in the interest of good international relations, I would keep people from Japan together, and though you could not smell sushi or sashimi, somehow I could conjure up images of their favorite dishes when entering a floor that they might be on.

The Japanese gentleman that narrowly escaped death at the hands of, or should I say at the body of the *pixie*, was an individual whom I had previously befriended. Thinking about him brings to mind a somewhat interesting, cultural, learning experience that I had. This banker was a lonely, single, gentleman who yearned for the company of a friendly countrywoman. He was so shook up after the unfortunate death of

Miss. Kadash that I felt it would nice if I could do something for Mr. Watanabe.

One early evening, upon greeting him in the lobby, I mentioned a young female guest who was from his country. To my surprise, he had never met Miss. Kiyoko Teshigawara, a guest who resided on the same floor that he was on. Try to remember her surname; at the opportune time I could not. His eyes opened wide with delight when I told him I would see if she was in. I called her room, told her it was Mr. Sokol, the manager, and that I would love to have her meet a countryman, a fine gentleman who was also a guest in the hotel. She was pleased to hear this and accepted my invitation to come down to the lobby to meet him.

Before long the elevator doors opened and Kiyoko demurely exited and headed in my direction. I stood between the two as they acknowledged each other and bowed. They looked at each other again and then they each bowed again. They repeated this four times and now, looking distressed, glanced at me for help. I was at a loss. Then a bulb went off in my head—I realized that I had not formerly introduced them. Actually, I couldn't introduce them because I could not remember her name, (do you?) and even if I did, I certainly couldn't pronounce it. I raced quickly to the front desk and from the guest rack retrieved the card with her name on it.

Returning to them I said, "Mr. Watanabe, this is ... " and pointed to her name.

He smiled and said "Miss. Teshigawara, it is a pleasure to meet you." and they finally stopped bowing.

They left the hotel together for dinner or whatever. I felt a sense of relief, as well as satisfaction, in knowing that I had done a good deed and even perhaps had initiated a meaningful relationship.

* * *

This recollection brings to mind another cute incident involving individuals from Japan. I tried hard over the years to introduce the hotel to neighboring corporations. One of corporations that I had made a presentation to was Kobe Steel. In response to my presentation, they called one day to inquire if a visiting executive from Japan could stop by to see our accommodations. Since the executive spoke very little English, a manager from the New York office, who was fluent in English, would accompany him.

"Absolutely," I replied. "I would be delighted to extend any courtesies to the gentlemen and will certainly show them all the various units that are available."

The caller said they would arrive in about forty-five minutes. I grabbed a reference book in which I had highlighted certain salutary expressions in Japanese and I reviewed some of them. Forty-five minutes later, as I was standing in the lobby, I saw two Japanese gentlemen enter. I greeted them and then asked them to join me, as I held the elevator doors open. They entered the car and I followed them in.

I pushed the twelfth floor button and then turned to the executive and said "Ohayo."

He smiled at me, hesitated and then said, "Cincinnati."

I paused, looked at him questioningly and again said, "Ohayo."

He seemed somewhat confused, looked at his New York counterpart and responded with, "Cleveland."

I didn't have to be a rocket scientist to figure out that I was digging a hole for myself, so I shut up and just showed them our rooms. They were extremely pleased and secured a room for the Japanese executive. Afterward, the New York counterpart took me aside and explained that in a formal situation, one should say Ohayo Gozaimasu. One would say Ohayo only if you were familiar with the person. Luckily I did not create an international disaster.

THE ASYLUM IS FILLING UP - 10ᵀᴴ FLOOR

Perhaps my expectation level exceeded reality. No one believed that the high occupancy rates would continue after the 1965 World's Fair, but I don't think we imagined business would deteriorate as much as it did. Each year afterward, we experienced less and less transient business. Even the extended stay bookings diminished. By the summer of 1971, I was foreseeing doomsday again. Normally during the summer season we were slow, but this year our occupancy was down to 65% and there were no reservations in the book. There was nothing more that I could do; every attempt to stimulate more traffic ended in futility.

It was a hot, muggy Sunday afternoon. I had read the *New York Times* front to back and was looking forward, with great anticipation, to spending the evening at home with Annette and the kids. Suddenly a black stretch limousine pulled up under our marquee. The chauffeur quickly jumped out and opened the door for what I hoped would be a new guest. Wow, this was exciting!

A woman in her fifties slipped gracefully from the safe confines of the limousine, wearing the most unusual attire for an August heat wave. She was clothed in a raccoon coat that almost reached the ground with a matching fur hat. Her hands were hidden in a huge, raccoon muff and as she walked closer, her high fur boots came into view. Barely visible beneath her hat and turned up collar was a pale face devoid of make-up and which obviously had never seen the sun.

Since the bellman was probably sleeping in the baggage room, I walked out to greet her. Extending my hand, I introduced myself.

She countered with, "I'm Mrs. Daniels, I don't have a reservation, but hopefully you can accommodate me."

Little did she know that on that day I could have handled one hundred walk-ins. She signed the register and I buzzed Lincoln, hoping he was not in too deep a sleep and would respond quickly. He did. I handed him the key to room 1011 and asked him to take our new guest, Mrs. Daniels, and her belongings to her room. Maybe things were looking up. She did, however, appear extremely eccentric in all that fur at this time of year. I had a feeling, deep in my gut, that she would be a new guest of the Asylum.

The following morning, a message from Mrs. Daniels was waiting for me. She asked me to please call her. I undertook this chore immediately—I certainly did not want to lose a valued transient guest.

"Good morning Mrs. Daniels, this is Mr. Sokol, the Manager. Is there anything I can do for you?"

"Yes, I would like another room."

"Mrs. Daniels, I am terribly sorry that you are unhappy with your room, I'll send Lincoln up immediately to move you to a more preferable one."

"Mr. Sokol, perhaps you don't understand. I don't want to be moved, **I want another room.**"

Scratching my head, I tried to decipher this request. She wants another room but doesn't want to be moved into it. Perhaps she was having guests. I asked her to come down and sign the register for room 1010. She did this immediately. The morning after this, there was another message waiting for me. I could hardly believe it—Mrs. Daniels wanted yet another room. I assigned her 1009. Keep in mind, this was summertime and half of the tenth floor was available.

By the end of the week her requests sounded more frantic. "**I must have another room immediately!**"

Ultimately, we had one guest paying for seven rooms at a transient rate. Ten more guests like this and I would be able to raise the dividends to the partners.

THE INVENTION - 10TH FLOOR

Every morning at 11 o'clock, dressed in her summer fur ensemble (I wondered what her winter ensemble looked like), Mrs. Daniels would walk out of the hotel into her waiting limousine. She would always return in the late afternoon. I couldn't imagine where this eccentric woman went everyday. I checked with Bella to find out if Mrs. Daniels had any interesting calls—knowing full well that Mom probably eavesdropped on them. According to Mom, she had no calls and no visitors. One thing that I did notice, however, was that the bellmen were extremely attentive to her.

One Friday, Mrs. Daniels called with the following request, "Mr. Sokol could you please debit my account $15 and give this amount to the bellman, Joseph?

Every few days the same call was repeated. Finally, I asked Joseph what was going on and why he was receiving so much money from her.

He explained, "Mrs. Daniels keeps asking me to buy her batteries. The batteries cost $5 and she always give me a $10 tip."

My curiosity was overwhelming! Of course, being the dedicated worker that I was, it was important for

187

me to get to know our guest as best I could—I certainly did not want to jeopardize the income from seven rooms. In addition, there was always the possibility of an entrepreneurial opportunity that I wouldn't want to overlook. So ... I called Mrs. Daniels and asked if I could chat with her in private. She granted me an audience and I quickly sped up to her *suite of rooms*. I had to knock at four doors before I finally located her.

I performed many menial and labor-intensive activities while working in the hotel but I always wore a suit, starched dress shirt, and tie. For this meeting, I was definitely over-dressed. What I really needed was the white jacket worn in the psycho wards.

Mrs. Daniels proceeded to tell me about her problems since checking into the hotel. Apparently, without my knowledge, Con Edison was performing repairs and construction in the nearby streets. Their activity was generating and emitting radiation that was permeating the hotel walls. After her first night's stay, she needed another room to bathe in. The next day there was radiation in the second room also, so she again needed a different room, followed by the next day and so on. There was no logic or rational to what she said. I thought, why keep the old rooms if they are filled with radiation? Of course, I didn't ask her this. I had to protect my revenue. Shifting gears, I asked her about the battery purchases.

She looked at me as if I just landed from Mars, and replied, "Don't you know that light deflects radiation? I need the batteries for ... "

She opened the dresser drawer and displayed about twenty-five flashlights. Looking at all those flashlights—

my mind quickly reverted back to a night five years ago. Can you imagine how useful those flashlights would have been if we had access to them the night of the blackout?

Suddenly a great idea popped into my mind and I needed to prepare for it so I quickly excused myself and left. I went to Rite Aid and purchased a pair of large, horn-rimmed sunglasses. When I returned to the hotel, I told Bella and the desk clerk that I had an important project to complete downstairs and did not want to be disturbed except for an emergency.

Earlier I mentioned that I had replaced the General Manager and the Auditor. In addition, I established a workshop and after butchering a few televisions, air conditioners, and refrigerators, I managed, with the help of Ernie, to maintain and repair the surviving appliances. I now had a fairly sophisticated shop—one that would certainly enable me to complete this not too complex project.

I labored over it an entire day while the desk clerk took care of the day-to-day business. When my project was completed, I anxiously rang the phones in all seven rooms and finally located Mrs. Daniels. I told her it was imperative that I see her. There had been a scientific breakthrough and I was anxious to discuss it with her. Without questioning, she summoned me to immediately meet her in 1006.

I didn't have to knock on her door because she was in the hallway, waiting for me with great anticipation. "What have they discovered?"

I slowly unwrapped the glasses that I had been laboring over and put them on. Then I slipped my hand into my pocket and pressed a button. Miraculously, two little lights, at the corners of the frame, lit up.

She gasped and said, "**That's unbelievable**."

I told her there was more to it. I continued explaining that when she was out walking in the evening and needed to change directions upon reaching a corner, all she would have to do was press either the right or left button and the glasses would serve as directional signals.

"I must have them! How much are they?"

I told her the glasses were still in beta test, but when on the market they would sell for $3,000 each. The price didn't even faze her.

"I'll order 3 pair. Please get them to me quickly."

Returning to my office I began to think. There was no way that I would take money from an obviously sick woman. But I wondered what prompted me to initiate this farce to begin with? Where did the $3,000 number come from? Perhaps it started out with the thought of an entrepreneurial opportunity. I always liked to build things. Perhaps this was an opportunity to build something novel and unique? Was I searching for a way to assuage my boredom? Or did I just cross the line and become an inmate in this asylum?

Upon further introspection I was able to identify other catalysts, besides the above, for my behavior. Both my father and his younger sister, Shirley, had not only the desire, but also the talent and presence to be on stage. My Aunt Shirley, in her senior years at Century Village in Deerfield Beach, Florida, would stand center stage and do a one-hour, ever changing, hysterically funny monologue in front of audiences of hundreds. My dad would relish entertaining groups by singing cantorial selections and/or modern day pop music. I guess some of their genes were passed on to me and now, perhaps I had found my own personal stage in the hotel. There could be no other explanation for my participation in the Daniels' dramas. It certainly wasn't for financial gain.

* * *

There are quite a few additional stories that involved Mrs. Daniels, but first I must tell you what happened after I took the glasses home that evening. I handed the glasses to my son, David, who was now five years old. I told him that I made him a new toy and showed him how it worked. The following day he gleefully went out to demonstrate his new toy to his friends. Among his friends, unbeknownst to me, was the son of a toy manufacturer. You can guess the rest of the story. To rub salt in the wound, the battery-operated glasses (exaggeratedly enlarged) became one of the top-sellers that season, "Zany Zappers." Apparently, I was successful, I did create something novel and unique ... too bad I couldn't share in the profits!

THE DETECTIVE CONFRONTS RADIATION - 10TH FLOOR

If you met Mrs. Daniels, indoors, I don't think you would easily notice her problems or idiosyncrasies. However, after a while, I became aware that she could easily be distracted and had either a short attention span or short-term memory loss. For example, while standing in front of her I could introduce myself as Mr. Sokol, the General Manager, and then a moment later just by placing a hat on my head, reintroduce myself as Peter Pan and she would believe me. There were many Mrs.

Daniels episodes, but the most memorable ones seem to be those that I had completely thrust myself into. The following is a case in point.

One morning Bella rang my office phone and with an anxious voice said, "Herby, I am very worried that Mrs. Daniels might have serious problems."

"What kind of problems, Mom?"

"I don't know but she asked me to get her the name of a detective."

"Don't worry; I'll take care of it."

I called Mrs. Daniels and asked, "Is there anything I can do to make your stay more comfortable?"

"Yes, would you please get me a detective?"

"Is anyone bothering you? Perhaps I could help you?"

"No, just please get me a detective; I have to go to the bank."

"But Mrs. Daniels, I could send a staff member to accompany you to the bank. You don't have to go to the trouble of engaging the services of a detective." I couldn't wait to hear her response.

"You don't understand, the bank has **yellow** carpeting, and it's full of radiation! Please get me a detective who has a Geiger counter, and make sure he brings it with him. I will need his services tomorrow morning at 11:55."

Well, I did try to dissuade her from hiring a detective. Subconsciously though, I kept wondering if it was possible that I didn't want to discourage her need for a detective? After all, I could play a detective and I did have a Geiger counter.

Okay, you're wondering why I would have a Geiger counter—let me explain. After the Cuban Missile Crisis in 1962, New York City's preparations for nuclear war intensified. Hotels were designated as fall-out shelters and they were stockpiled with supplies that included: water drums, medical supplies, bitter tasting ration crackers, and other necessary items ... one of which was a Geiger counter. Of course, our Geiger counter was no longer operable and even if it was, I certainly didn't have the slightest idea how to operate it. Maybe some of Mrs. Daniels' batteries would help.

The next morning at 11:55 I was fully decked out playing *The Detective*. Wearing a black trench coat with a turned-up-collar, a Humphrey Bogart fedora, and carrying my yellow Geiger counter, I took the elevator to the tenth floor. I removed my hat and knocked on five of her seven doors until I finally located the detective's client.

"Who is it?" she called through the door.

"It's Mr. Sokol, the General Manager."

Mrs. Daniels quickly opened the door and greeted me, "Good Morning, Mr. Sokol. Is my detective here?"

"Yes," I said, as I quickly moved away from the door and put on my fedora. "Here he is."

She looked me over (swiftly forgetting that Mr. Sokol had initially knocked) and started to walk me through the next hour and half's schedule. I guess I got the part, because we then took the elevator down to the lobby and passed through the front doors to a waiting stretch limousine. The chauffeur opened the door for her and instructed me to sit up front with him.

He asked for my name, and I responded, "I'm the detective."

It was a little after noon as we drove up Fifth Avenue, somewhere in the mid-forties. The streets were filled with workers on their lunch break, business executives heading to luncheon meetings, and shoppers milling about the sidewalks and storefront windows. Traffic was horrendous with taxis maneuvering and car horns honking. I started to feel stage fright. I was tempted to bail out and run *off stage*.

Just then, the chauffeur pulled up in front of a large bank. He quickly jumped out, opened the door for Mrs. Daniels, and then called to me to come over and walk in front of her. Try to imagine this scene—a hot, muggy summer day; Fifth Avenue teeming with pedestrian traffic; a short man carrying a Geiger counter, wearing a trench coat with a turned up collar, and a fedora; followed closely by a woman clad entirely in raccoon from head to foot; and a chauffeured stretch limousine dutifully waiting.

There I was center stage with an audience of a few dozen, curious people stopping to stare at us. Who could blame them; I would too. We entered the bank and as we stepped onto the yellow carpet, I could sense that Mrs. Daniels was shuddering. She instructed me to head for the staircase and lead her down to the vault area where a bank clerk sat at her desk. Mrs. Daniels greeted her and signed in. However, when the bank employee told Mrs. Daniels that I could not accompany her into the vault because I wasn't listed on the registration card, my client immediately erupted with a loud emotional outburst.

She screamed, "**If your bank kept the damn radiation out, I wouldn't have required the assistance of a detective to begin with!**"

The clerk's eyes opened wide with amazement. She realized that the woman was in a very distressed state and to placate her, she granted me permission and led us both into the vault area.

Mrs. Daniels asked me to check the safety deposit box for radiation before she opened it. I did as directed. Con Ed must have taken a vacation day—the area was clean in every respect. She unlocked the box and asked me to carry it into one of the small rooms. I carried the box and the Geiger counter into a small room that was sparsely furnished with a table and two chairs.

Sitting down, she instructed me to remove the contents and place it on the table. I did so and quickly moved aside. I started to feel extremely uncomfortable. It was one thing to accompany her, as a detective, but I didn't want to be involved with her personal affairs. Without counting, I could tell that there had to be hundreds of thousands of dollars in Bearer Bonds. Feeling extremely uncomfortable, I told Mrs. Daniels that I had another case that required my services, and that I would have to leave soon.

She said, "We will leave right after I have a quick meeting with my accountant and my attorney."

A wave of panic suddenly swept over me. How could I explain what I was doing? **What was I doing?** I didn't have to worry for long. Mrs. Daniels quickly finished her chores and accompanied me, as I carried the box back and returned it to the appointed slot.

As we left the vault area, she pointed in the direction of a closed door and instructed me to lead the way. We walked across the hall and I opened the door for my client. We entered a very impressive meeting room. In the center was a large, cherry wood conference table surrounded by many chairs. Immediately two gentlemen sprang to their feet. They glanced at Mrs. Daniels and then quizzically looked at me (a man carrying a Geiger counter). In unison they both greeted her and then the younger one turned to me and questioned who I was.

I responded in a strong authoritative voice, "I am the detective and who are you gentlemen?

The older of the two stammered, "I am Elliot K—Katz, Mrs. D—Daniels' account—tant, and m—my colleague is S—Sam Herman, her attorney."

I could swear both were simultaneously turning green. We all sat down and they had their meeting. I don't know what they discussed; all I know was that my head was spinning with thoughts of how to escape.

We left about fifteen minutes later, carefully following the same procession. I led with my Geiger counter and Mrs. Daniels followed behind me. We crossed the dangerous "yellow carpet" in the expansive main banking area, past the bewildered audience, went out the doors, and finally entered into the safety of the limousine. As I climbed into my designated seat, I sighed with relief and prayed that we'd return to the hotel without further incident or inquisition. I breathed deeply and tried to calm down.

Upon our return Mrs. Daniels inquired, "What is your fee for today?"

I replied, "There is no charge, my time was paid for by the hotel as a courtesy to you."

"Please do thank Mr. Sokol for me," she replied.

I don't want to appear judgmental, but the reactions of the accountant and the lawyer to the detective, led me to believe that they were taking financial advantage of my client. But, that was not my concern, I had an asylum to run; and what an asylum it was!

DESTRUCTION BY RADIATION - 10ᵀᴴ FLOOR

A few weeks after my last encounter with Mrs. Daniels, I received a frantic call from her pleading for help. She sounded terrified and was apparently in some imminent danger. My initial instinct was to jump up from my desk and rush to help her. But, I quickly remembered who was at the other end of the phone and instead I just tried to reassure and pacify her by saying that everything would be okay. I promised her that I would be up soon.

"Mr. Sokol, this is urgent, I need help NOW!"

Frightened by the desperation in her voice, I no longer hesitated and informed her that I was on my way.

She was waiting for me in the hallway outside the door. The woman was in an agitated state, trembling and sobbing. She motioned to me to open the door and look inside. I boldly walked in and gave the room a cursory glance while examining the window, walls and ceiling. Absolutely nothing appeared disturbed, wrong, or unusual. I could have suggested that she move to one of the other six rooms she was paying for, but she was too distraught to be even slightly rational.

"What's wrong Mrs. Daniels?"

"Don't you see the walls? They're blasted away! The radiation blew gaping holes in them."

Okay, I could handle this situation. I said, "Mrs. Daniels, please follow my instructions carefully and I will take care of everything. Come with me."

I put my arm around her trembling body and slowly walked her back into the room.

I continued, "My construction manager, Tom O'Malley, will be up immediately and will repair and fortify your room against the radiation. I need you to go into the bathroom and lock the door. There will be a lot of dust and debris flying about, but you will be safe in the bathroom."

Out of fear, she followed my directions and secured herself in the bathroom. I opened the entry door and neatly placed my jacket and tie on the corridor floor and then loudly slammed the door. The imaginary Tom O'Malley entered! After a few moments, I started to pound the wall next to the bathroom ... **Thud, Whack, Slam** the wall resounded. I moved up and down the wall pounding until my fists were hurting. Then I waited for a minute or two and started to pound the adjacent wall ... **Smash, Bang, Boom** this wall echoed. After stopping to rest for a moment or so, I picked up my imaginary trowel (actually I used my American Express card) and carefully smoothed out the pretend plaster ... **Scratch, Scrape** first on one wall and then on the next. I certainly didn't want the plaster to dry with bumps and lumps!

Finally I approached the bathroom door and told Mrs. Daniels, "You can come out now. It's okay; all the holes are fixed."

She did so hesitatingly, still gripped with fear.

The woman looked around her surroundings and exclaimed, "Mr. O'Malley this is unbelievable! I can't even see the repair marks. Everything is like new. Thank you so much, and please thank Mr. Sokol for me."

Another calamity was resolved successfully. I can't imagine what I would do without my magical powers.

The Aluminum Pan Mummy -
10ᵀᴴ Floor

A few weeks later Bella greeted me with another problem concerning Mrs. Daniels. She had called down to the switchboard requesting a moving service. This was puzzling to me since she arrived in a chauffeured limousine and checked in carrying only an overnight suitcase. During her stay, she had not purchased any furniture or bulky items that I was aware of. It would really be a shame, as well as a blow to our revenue stream, to lose seven transient rooms. But I wasn't sure which would be worse, losing the revenue or not knowing why she needed a mover. Let's face it; curiosity was getting the better of me. I called her multiple residences and after six tries located her in room 1010. I introduced myself as Ollie the mover, referred by Mr. Sokol.

Mrs. Daniels inquired, "Could you have a van available for me tomorrow morning at 11?"

"Of course."

It was imperative that I learn of her plans, and hopefully, subtly dissuade her from leaving. The next morning at 8, I was at Avis renting a van. Promptly at 11 A.M. I was at one of her doors attired in Levis, t-shirt, sneakers, and a New York Yankees baseball cap.

205

She answered the door, ushered me in and then stood in the center of the room visibly anxious to leave her seven-room suite. Her packed suitcase was standing on the floor next to the kitchenette and on the bed were stuffed shopping bags. She was ready to go but I sensed something was missing. I stood there puzzled and then it dawned on me ... she was not wearing her fur ensemble. For the first time since I knew her, she would be braving the ravages of radiation without her protection. Snapping back to my Ollie responsibilities, I asked which furniture pieces were to be moved.

"Mr. Ollie, I have no furniture. I need you to move *me*. I can no longer stay at The Roger Williams Hotel. The radiation is much too severe here and it's taking a toll on my health."

"But Mrs. Daniels, why do you need my van? A taxi would have been sufficient for a small suitcase and a few shopping bags."

Her response stunned me, "I am checking into an apartment hotel on Park Avenue. **I need you to pack me up and deliver me**. In the shopping bags I have aluminum pans and duct tape to keep the pans in place."

She continued to explain exactly what I was to do. I have to tell you that it took a great deal of self-control not to end up on the floor, doubled up in hysterical laughter. Thankfully, I was able to control myself. So I followed her instructions—I removed the aluminum pie pans, aluminum baking pans, and rolls of duct tape from the shopping bags. I then proceeded to wrap her from head to foot until she was completely encased with pans that were held in place with the tape. When I was finally finished, she resembled an aluminum mummy. The rigidity of the pans and tape prevented her from sitting or walking. She could only take teeny, tiny, bunny hops. I called Lincoln, and asked him to come to room 1010 to assist me. In addition, I warned him to keep a straight face when he saw our departing guest. When Lincoln came up and entered the room, he froze in place at the sight of the *mummy*. He just stood there transfixed—his eyes bulging and his jaw hanging.

I said to Lincoln, "Grab the suitcase, and we'll both assist Mrs. Daniels to the elevator."

He snapped out of it, picked up the suitcase and with his other arm tried to support one side of Mrs. Daniels. I put one arm on her back, and with the other arm I tried to keep her erect. We then gently pushed her forward while she tried to propel herself with her teeny bunny hops. I started thinking ... if we continued at this pace I might be compelled to bill her for another night's stay. Finally, we got into the elevator and started our descent. As the elevator approached the lobby, I prayed that it would be empty. This was the only time that I thought it would be a blessing to have a summer lull and be half empty. As the elevator door opened, I saw with a quick glance that I would be spared embarrassment. Except for Bella, who stood there with her mouth agape, and the desk clerk who looked like he was in shock, there was no one to witness Mrs. Daniels in her designer Alcoa ensemble, jumping and sliding to the front door and the waiting van.

She was right; she really did require a van. She could not sit on a seat; she could not bend. Lincoln and I opened the back doors, tilted the rigid soon to be exguest and slid her in. Of course, Lincoln would have to accompany me to make the delivery. I, alone, could not handle removing her and bunny hopping her into her new residence. Besides, in the event that the police should stop me, I needed a witness to attest to the fact that I was not a kidnapper, but just a *Good Samaritan* hotel manager. We reached the Park Avenue address in about fifteen minutes. Leaving the vehicle running, I went to the hotel reception desk and informed the clerk that I had brought their new guest, Mrs. Daniels. He inquired as to where she was.

"She's in the back of the van."

With a quizzical expression he asked, "Why doesn't she come in?"

"You'll have to go out and see for yourself."

Now, he looked apprehensive and proceeded to leave his post at the desk and walked outside to the van. Lincoln opened the van's back doors for him and he looked in. I cannot, to this day, dispel from memory the startled look on this man's face when he saw his new guest.

After regaining his composure, he sharply exclaimed, **"She can not come in through the front entrance!"**

Since Mrs. Daniels had prepaid for her stay, the management of her new residence hotel could not legally deny her access. Lincoln and I had to hop/slide her through the service entrance to deliver her to her new apartment. After escorting her upstairs and unwrapping her, we bid her farewell and wished her nothing but happiness and a radiation-free stay in her new home. By the way, I did bill her for the cost of the van.

The Start of my New Beginning

A month or so before Mrs. Daniels had checked out, a young man had walked into the lobby and asked for the manager. I went out to greet him, and he introduced himself as Paul Gold, a New York University Law School student. He told me that he had access to many students who required dormitory facilities and that he would be able to bring them to my hotel for a small fee. I thanked him and bid him adieu. There was no way I would turn the hotel, even just a floor or two, into a college dorm. Two weeks later another young man visited. He introduced himself as Richard Fogel, a New York University student, and Paul Gold's partner. He was brash, overly cocky and insulting. He implied that our hotel was a dump and he could save it. I threw him out bodily.

Truthfully, business was so slow that I dreaded going to work each day and to top it off, we had now lost the revenue of the seven rooms that Mrs. Daniels had been renting. I dragged myself in every day; however, I was arriving later and later each morning. Soon I was getting in at 11A.M. Waiting for me one morning were the two college entrepreneurs. I was not in any mood to be insulted again and tried to dismiss them.

Paul suggested, "Look, let's sit down over coffee and discuss the possibilities."

We did. The two virtually guaranteed me $150,000 in receipts for which they would receive 10% commission. They promised that the hotel would not be physically abused and that there would be no disruptive behavior from the students ... because both of them would be moving in (rent-free) to make sure everything was under control. The only thing that I had to do was order inexpensive bunk beds, which would provide the students with more room for desks and living area in each room.

I sat there and thought about this for a while. A week or two ago, I had felt I would never turn even a few floors into a dorm ... but I had to face reality. What did I have to lose? The hotel was in bad financial straits. I would be a fool not to try and do something to build up revenue. Hopefully, these two young men would be able to keep the students under control as they had promised.

We reached an agreement and our new residents started to arrive within days. It was the beginning of a new school year. Not only were there students from N.Y.U. but also from the Fashion Institute of Technology and quite a few from the American Academy of Dramatic Arts. Most of the students were women, much to the delight (and possible planning) of my two *policemen*. It was as promised. We derived new income, and the young women brought a feeling of rejuvenation to the hotel and smiles to the faces of our two young entrepreneurs.

Though the younger of the two was brash and sometimes intolerable, I seemed to gravitate to him more than to his partner. I guess Richard was more outgoing and friendly. As I got to know him better, I discovered that he was extremely bright, fearless and possessed a Type A personality. He seemed to be driven with a burning desire to succeed—quickly.

I questioned him once about this, and he replied, "Herb, I have to move quickly, because I don't believe I will live much past my thirtieth birthday."

MAGIC FINGERS - ROOM 707

It now seemed that everything, including life, was moving rapidly. Annette and I celebrated our fifteenth wedding anniversary, our oldest daughter, Sharyn became a Bat Mitzvah, and I was soon going to celebrate my thirteenth year at the Roger Williams. I guess the old adage is true, "Time flies when you're having fun". The hotel was now doing reasonably well. Assaults on my body and person ceased, and the asylum was unusually tranquil. Everything was moving forward with what seemed to be its own inertia.

Over the last few years we had bought out our limited partners, changed our company into a Subchapter S corporation, and raised our dividends significantly. We were also able to refurnish most of the 216 rooms with new televisions, modern furniture, carpeting, as well as new draperies with coordinated bedspreads.

I just didn't have the heart to discard the old furniture, which consisted primarily of wooden drop-down secretary desks, dressers and end tables. I took one of the secretary desks home, and after Annette refinished it in a deep reddish, antique finish, it looked beautiful in Jodi's bedroom. I moved the rest of these antiques into the hotel's fourth floor storage area, a substantially large unusable space over the church. Little did I know how fortuitous this decision would turn out to be.

In addition to new furnishings, I also placed *Magic Fingers* into most of the transient rooms. This was a somewhat innovative device for that period. It was a self-contained motor that attached to the bed's box-spring coils and would vibrate considerably, when a quarter was placed into its attached coin box.

Remembering the following always brings a smile to my face. There was a call girl who was a guest in the hotel at that time. (Of course, I knew what her vocation was because of Mom's due-diligence.) Her name was Miss. Marlowe and she was quite beautiful. The woman was an absolute clone of Patricia Medina, a popular, voluptuous, exotic leading lady of British films at the time. According to Mom, she did her limited consulting activities strictly off premises and her beauty and wardrobe were such that we looked forward to her comings and goings.

As it was my responsibility to empty the coin boxes in the rooms, I had on quite a few occasions entered Miss. Marlowe's room (with her permission), during her off-business hours. I always found her resting in bed in a kind of ecstatic stupor. With each passing day, it seemed to me that she spent more and more time lying there in her suspended state. This definitely was limiting her productive working hours. I would like to believe that my *Magic Fingers* were responsible for her ecstasy. Somehow, I suspected that I derived more revenue from her coin box than she earned from her consulting activities. It was with great regrets that I watched her check out, for not only did I lose room revenue, but I also lost the vicarious excitement derived from emptying her box.

CRISIS MANAGEMENT

On October 6, 1973, Egypt and Syria attacked Israel on Yom Kippur, starting the fourth Arab-Israeli War. Ten days later OPEC oil ministers agreed to use oil as a weapon to punish the West for its support of Israel and recommended an embargo against what they considered unfriendly States. They also mandated a cut in all exports. Two days later they proclaimed an embargo on all oil exports to the United States. I couldn't immediately project how the embargo would affect The Roger Williams Hotel, but it didn't take long to find out.

The world suddenly seemed to turn topsy-turvy. The embargo triggered a shock in the United States. The price of gasoline went from a national average of 38.5 cents to 55.1 cents in six months. Our economy was thrust into sudden inflation and economic recession. The Fed's response to the crisis was to implement price controls and rationing of gasoline, which only exacerbated the problem. Long lines suddenly appeared at service stations. It was possible to wait for hours on one of these lines, hoping that they didn't run out of gas before it was your turn to fill up. If your license plate number ended in an even number, you could only get gas on an even-numbered date, and the same held true for odd numbered plates. Year-round daylight saving time was implemented and calls went out for individuals and businesses to conserve energy. Ads like "Don't be Fuelish" could now be seen everywhere.

Our hotel burned #6 fuel oil and initially there were no problems in acquiring it. Eventually fuel delivery became spotty and unreliable. Our supplier seemed to have the fuel but somehow it was not reaching us in a timely fashion. This prompted me to start rationing heat and hot water. I was able to do this without too many complaints from tenants and guests. One day our fuel tank was at its bottom and our scheduled delivery did not arrive. I called the oil company and they sounded as frustrated as I was. They could not tell me when a delivery would be made. Determined as I was, I saw no clear options to avoid the loss of heat and hot water to our guests.

It was then that I had a vision—the fourth floor was stocked with our old furniture. Could I do this? It probably wasn't legal, but I rationalized that, in this situation, the comfort of our guests was far more important than any infraction of environmental laws.

I put together a team of workers armed with hand trucks and all of us proceeded to the fourth floor. We loaded up our hand trucks with furniture and in an endless caravan brought our potential fuel to the basement power plant. Ernie and I then proceeded to break up the furniture and fired up the furnace with our new source of fuel. Working all day and night we just kept throwing pieces of furniture into the furnace. We managed to keep our guests comfortably warm, with enough hot water for bathing. Fortunately, our fuel delivery arrived early the next day.

The crises ended a few months later on March 17, 1974 to be exact. Life returned to normal ... for most New Yorkers. Mine returned to its usual chaotic state with the now accustomed weirdness accepted as normal.

MOON OVER MANHATTAN

One evening a few weeks later, Miss. Katherine Pearson, a monthly tenant in room 714, calmly placed a plastic bag over her head and retired for the evening. We discovered this the next day, when the maids went to service her room ... another suicide had taken place. Miss. Pearson was a matronly looking woman, about sixty years of age, and appeared, at least on the surface, to be emotionally stable. She comported herself in a friendly and considerate manner. There were internal hotel rumors floating about that Ernie was very friendly with her and some went as far as to suggest that he was *servicing* her. The coroner ruled her death a suicide and a few months later, we discovered that she had left all her worldly belongings to Ernie.

* * *

Maybe it was the full moon phenomenon. Four weeks after Miss. Pearson committed suicide ... a weekly guest, Mrs. Trovati, was found dead in the bathtub of room 507. I always thought of this as the "Foul Play Tub Death" since, to the best of my knowledge, the actual cause of her death was never determined.

When a death occurs at a hotel, procedure is to notify the police immediately. In most instances the room would then be sealed until clearance from the coroner's office and/or the police. This could take days ... creating a negative cash flow from that room. In this case, three officers arrived at the hotel not long after they were contacted. They asked to be taken to the deceased's room and I escorted them to room 507. I was then told that they had a lot of investigatory work to perform and the trio subsequently dismissed me.

I went back to my office to pay some bills. However, I couldn't dispel, from my mind, the horrible image of the dead woman lying naked in a tub full of cold water. I also fretted about the potential lost revenue from a prime corner accommodation. Being overly curious about the future status of this room, I went back upstairs and while standing outside the door, just happened to eavesdrop on the conversation of the policemen.

"Hey, Pete, look at these coins."

"Yeah, they look like mint condition. I wonder what they are worth?"

"Put them in the bag with the cash and jewelry."

I guess I was still naïve; it really upset me to hear these cops, who were supposed to be investigating a possible crime, actually enjoying themselves searching for the spoils. From previous conversations with Mrs. Trovati, I knew she had no living relatives; the police certainly did not. Notwithstanding this, I thought it quite improper for these policemen to end up as heirs of her estate. Becoming incensed, I used my passkey and again entered the room.

"Hey guys, are you almost done here?"

"We're just waiting for the meat wagon."

As the cop finished blurting out his statement, Lincoln led the Medical Examiner's team into the room. One hour later, with the preliminary investigation completed and the body removed, a crime scene tape was placed on the door.

Returning to the lobby I was told that Miss. Flanagan had a problem she wanted to discuss with me. I prayed we didn't have another bow and arrow slinger hiding out in a room. I went down to the basement and proceeded to the laundry room.

"Good morning," I said with trepidation.

Miss. Flanagan looked up and with a concerned voice answered, "Good morning, Mr. Sokol. Sorry to bother you but I have a problem with the towels and I was hoping that maybe you could help."

Miss. Flanagan managed the laundry for the hotel and for some inexplicable reason, the clean towels were emerging from the washer with a grayish color. I got fully involved in attempting to solve our towel issue. After dealing with this problem for almost an hour and not finding a solution, I thought, what the hell, maybe I'll just paint the bathrooms gray; that way the towels will match. In any event, I left the problem in the capable hands of Miss. Flanagan. I was getting hungry.

I really needed to escape from this morning's crises so I decided to take a walk to "The Old Garden" on East 28th Street. Actually, if I had my druthers, I would have gotten out of town all together. It was a refreshing spring day and it felt good to get out of the hotel and go for a long walk and clear my head. "The Old Garden" was a cozy, dimly lit bistro. More importantly, I really needed a drink.

As I entered, I was recognized and greeted by Frank, one of the waiters, "Another bad morning, Mr. Sokol?"

I didn't have to answer, as soon as I ordered a double Dewar's on the rocks, he knew. As I sipped the scotch I could feel it warming my insides. I started to calm down a little. That's when I remembered that I was still hungry. Time to order lunch.

"Frank, I'll have eggs ala russe for an appetizer and an open sliced turkey sandwich with lots of gravy and mashed potatoes."

Annette will be so envious when I tell her where I went for lunch today, I thought. This was one of her favorite Manhattan restaurants. I'm not sure if she liked it for its ambience or the eggs ala russe; maybe it was a combination of both. Frank brought my appetizer which was actually hard boiled eggs, cut in half, sitting on a bed of Romaine lettuce, covered with what I believe was Russian dressing, and sprinkled with crumbled bacon. This was Annette's and my favorite appetizer (we weren't worried about cholesterol then). I left over half of the turkey sandwich. I had had my fill. Besides, now that I had some protein and alcohol in me, I felt fortified enough to return to work.

When I entered my office, thoughts and images of Mrs. Trovati overwhelmed me again. I told Mom I was going upstairs to examine room 507. I ducked under the crime scene tape and entered the room. An uneasy, creepy sensation came over me. It was as if I felt her presence in the room. In between the windows facing 31st Street was a bookcase laden with texts and nonfiction books. Standing prominently on the top shelf was a gold colored, leather bound Bible. Reaching up, I removed it from the shelf and started to leaf through the pages. Suddenly, I found a $100 bill stuck between two pages. I removed it and continued to leaf through the bible, maybe a little more quickly, curious to see if there were any other bills hidden in it. Another $100 bill appeared, which I also removed. Continuing my examination of this miraculous Bible, I discovered one more $100 bill. After concluding my bible study, I began a frenzied examination of the rest of the many books on the shelves. I removed each book from its place and painstakingly shook each one until my wrists ached from this maneuver. Unfortunately, there were no more miracles.

I would like to believe that Mrs. Trovati placed the bills in the bible, with the thought that upon her demise, the money would pass into the hands of someone who had respect for religion. It is interesting that the police, during their investigation, did not come across these bills. I really began to feel that the bills were put there for me. Riding down in the elevator, $300 richer, I prayed that these recent deaths were not the beginning of an epidemic.

THE TELEVISION REPAIRMAN - ROOM 610

Thinking about epidemics brings to mind this episode, which occurred in early June. Because I had an early morning meeting with the hotel partners, I didn't arrive at the hotel until after 11 A.M. Vince, our new desk clerk, quickly brought me up to date on items that required my personal attention such as: advance reservations, service issues, maintenance and some guest complaints.

"That's it, Herb; oh wait, there is something else that you should follow-up on. There are two women in 610 who paid in advance for their first night stay but are now two days in arrears. And could you please cover for me for five minutes; I ordered something from the coffee shop and I just want to pick it up."

As Vince left, I picked up the stack of registration cards and found what I was looking for. The two women were Janice Peters and Mary O'Connor from Albany, N.Y. I asked Mom to connect me to room 610 and was immediately greeted by a sexy voice.

"Hello, Janice here."

"Miss. Peters this is Mr. Sokol, the General Manager. Are you and Miss. O'Connor checking out today?"

"No, we plan on staying in town for a few more days. We are loving our stay here."

"I'm very happy to hear that; could you please come down, at your convenience, and put some money on your account?"

"Absolutely. By the way, could you send someone up to fix the television? There are some shows that we must watch before 1 P.M."

" Certainly, I'll take care of it in a little while. Have a good day, Miss. Peters."

The simplest solution to the television request would be to ask Ernie to carry up a replacement, but I had none available. Since I was the television expert, I hoped that I could adjust the set and that would suffice. When Vince returned, I grabbed a screwdriver and went up to room 610.

I knocked on the door and the same sexy voice responded, "Come in."

Our room doors automatically locked upon closure. Apparently someone had adjusted the lock to remain open because when I pushed on the door, it opened freely. This room had a small foyer entrance, then a bath to the left, a kitchenette to the right, and a bedroom area past the kithenette.

As I past the kitchenette I saw the two young women, each sprawled out on a twin bed and each wearing a very revealing negligee. The television, which was on, looked like it was playing perfectly. The two young women seemed to be in the age range of eighteen to twenty-two; but I was then, and still am now, a very poor judge of age. Both were fairly attractive and I could not help but notice their shapely bodies. One was a blonde, the other a brunette ... neither of them was bleached!

"Excuse me. Who is Miss. Peters?"

"I am," replied the blonde.

"Miss. Peters, I am somewhat confused. Your television seems to be in perfect working order."

"Yes, that's what we want to talk to you about."

The next part of the conversation had me, a forty-year old man who was married for sixteen years, blushing with embarrassment. The two young women jumped off their respective beds and proceeded to offer me all kinds of exotic sexual favors ... if I would advance them the funds to pay for their previous two nights, plus this current one. I told them it was out of the question and I wanted them out of the hotel by 1 P.M. They left and I wrote off the two days' room charges with no regrets.

The following day I had a visit from an officer of the law, on behalf of social services. He was inquiring about our former guests, Miss. Peters and Miss. O'Conner. It turned out that these girls were runaways, not eighteen to twenty-two, but barely sixteen.

In addition, the policeman informed me, "These two young girls are responsible for a rampant gonorrhea epidemic that has been spreading throughout Manhattan's east and west sides."

I suspect they must have gotten many free night stays in hotels around the city, but thankfully my hotel was no longer their homeless shelter.

The New Beginning

It is interesting to observe how some people never waver from their pursuit of a predetermined goal or objective. They put one foot in front of the other and continue marching forward. Others, such as me move forward, take a step backward, then forward again and then could be diverted in an altogether different direction. I wasn't dissatisfied or unhappy with my situation; there were still many challenges for me. In addition, the hotel continued to captivate me with its unique aura. However, circumstances unfolded that brought drastic changes to my life and thrust me into a new world of adventures.

It was now September 1974, and we had started our fourth year of providing dormitory rooms for students. Our new and returning students seemed happy with their accommodations and appeared to be applying most of their exuberant energy into partying, and what remained, into their studies. Richard was now in his senior year at New York University; Paul had graduated N.Y.U. Law and was writing his first sports book.

Over the years I noticed that quite a few of the students sought to supplement their support allowances by finding part-time, as well as full-time employment.

Richard, being the point man for student housing, was deluged with pleas for employment help and being the ultimate opportunist conjured up a concept.

"Herb, let's form an employment opportunity club with membership dues of maybe $25 a year. Picture this ... we can provide our members with assistance in writing resumes and we can also do some research and then give them contact numbers of potential company employers. What do you think?"

It sounded like it wouldn't take up too much of my time, so I agreed to participate. The club was formed and we named it FOKOL (a combination of our two last names). We set up an office in room 210, one of the back rooms that was impossible to rent. In our new office, Richard met with FOKOL members and offered them employment assistance. His counsel leaned heavily on resume preparation and how to conduct oneself during interviews. He also provided leads on position opportunities (that he got from the want ads of the classified).

Once a month we offered seminars. We invited *Titans of Industry* to lecture on how to succeed. One of our renowned guest lecturers was Harold Goldstein (my cousin). He was the successful proprietor of a dry cleaning establishment. Another was Barry Sandler—a human resource professional who used the hotel for his assignations. In exchange for our discreetness and a choice room, he would occasionally give lectures to our FOKOL members. He even hired our most beautiful member ... however, I was never quite sure what her job description included.

It did not take long for our membership to start clamoring for less lip service and more hands-on direct help. To this end, Richard, not knowing where else to turn, started to contact employment agencies. One agency, in particular, was receptive to meeting qualified students. We introduced quite a few students to them, and surprisingly, a good number of them got jobs.

Two events subsequently occurred, that had a dramatic impact on my fate. The first: the owners of the employment agency called and invited both Richard and me to dinner. We thought this was interesting; *they* were doing us a favor, and yet *they* wanted to take us out to dinner. Shouldn't it have been the other way around?

We went to a fine steak restaurant and started the evening off with drinks. For an appetizer, I had escargot that had been removed from the shell and cooked in a delicious garlic sauce. All four of us ordered the same entrée—filet mignon. The steak was unbelievably tender and was accompanied by asparagus and delicious, twice baked potatoes. Throughout the meal the demeanor of the two agency partners was extremely upbeat. I ordered a chocolate soufflé for dessert, and to complement our desserts, our hosts ordered a round of Courvoisier. It was while sniffing and sipping this delightful cognac, that the elder of the two partners pulled out a sheet of paper from his ledger and proceeded to show us how many thousands of dollars our referrals had brought them. Richard and I tried not to over-react and took this information very matter-of-factly.

Restraining my excitement, I calmly responded with, "I'm really happy that we were able to help."

At least now we knew why they were entertaining us. We were downright shocked to find out that an employment agency could make so much money just from placing our students.

* * *

The second occurrence that would influence and heavily impact on my future was a chance meeting that took place in the hotel. Jack Moronne, a corporate officer of a large brokerage house, was standing in the lobby. Jack was a new guest, referred to us by the Roosevelt Hotel during an unusual sell-out night. At the same time, Bob Fischer, a broker from Chicago was milling about.

Jokingly, while glancing first at Jack and then at Bob, I said, "You two have a lot in common. You should get to know each other."

I then proceeded to introduce them. The two chatted briefly and left the hotel together. Months later, I saw Jack signing in at the front desk. I walked toward him while thinking ... it's not a sell-out night, what is he doing here? Perhaps he had a lobotomy and lost his way.

Jack looked up and recognizing me said, "I owe you; I really have to thank you. You saved me $25,000!"

"Anytime I can be of service, Jack ... but how did I save you $25,000?"

What he had to say was mind-boggling. He went on to explain that months ago, he was interviewing "search firms" to assist him in identifying someone with the exact credentials of Bob Fischer. The search fee would have been $25,000. I was taken aback and almost blurted out, you mean just by introducing business people to each other search firms earn big fees. My God, I thought, look at all the people we introduce on a daily basis. Later that evening, I related this encounter to Richard.

"That's it!" Richard said excitedly. "We have to capitalize on our students and the hotel contacts. We have to go into this business!"

* * *

Richard always exuded infectious positive vibes, but now he was soaring. The next day he contacted real estate agencies trying to find appropriate office space. He was successful and found a relatively inexpensive office site nearby. Other than perhaps hanging out a sign, The Madison Group (we had discussed potential company names and this one sounded appropriate), I really had no idea what we would be doing there.

The office was located two blocks north on Madison Avenue in an antique of a building. The space was adequate, but it looked so old and depressing that I felt embarrassed to have my name associated with any venture housed there. Believe it or not this building and the office, were in much worse shape than The Roger Williams Hotel at its worst. However, Richard had already signed the lease and occupancy was to begin the following Monday. So ... the place was ours.

I asked him to call Mr. Fishbein, the landlord, and find out if he could get permission to have access to the space the Friday before. Richard did and permission was granted. I immediately called Pepe and another houseman, and asked if they would want to earn extra money working for me, personally, over the weekend. Enthusiastically, they both accepted my offer.

That evening, after I came home from work, Annette and I went to Pergament (the Home Depot of yesteryear). We picked out carpeting for the entire office and paneling for the front office. Then my wife got this crazy idea—why not hang bright red shag carpeting on the wall of the reception area that was opposite the entrance door. This would definitely brighten up the space. So with Annette's urging, I bought some red shag carpeting. Now you may be thinking that the place would look like a whorehouse, but in 1974, red was a very popular decorating color and shag was designer chic. In addition to the carpeting, we also purchased paint, spackle, brushes, trowels, sandpaper, tackless, hammers, nails, the list just seemed to go on and on. Let's face it, we needed a lot of supplies for our renovation work and I was not comfortable taking inventory from the hotel. I made arrangements to pick up the carpeting and paneling on Saturday morning.

Deep down I think Annette must have always wanted to be an interior decorator; she had so much fun picking out paneling and carpeting, and making sure the paint had just the right hue. I guess I am a lucky man ... I have a wife that has always been supportive of anything that I have wanted to do, no matter how crazy it might sound.

While we were out shopping, Richard was doing the same. His project was to find inexpensive new or used furniture; we needed desks, chairs, and storage cabinets. I hoped we would end up making more money than we were investing in this project.

THE CONTRACTOR

Friday at 5 P.M. Pepe, the handyman, and I carried the supplies that I had previously purchased, into the new office and began renovations for The Madison Group. Richard met us at the office and we all went to work. We spackled, sanded, and painted the back room for a good part of the night. The next day, I brought the carpeting and paneling to Manhattan in a rented van. I also brought my son, David, who was now nine years old. At home, he always liked to help me with any construction or repair jobs that I had and he certainly didn't want to miss out on this exciting opportunity. David helped with the paneling. His job was to hammer nails into the paneling grooves. We also started installing the carpeting in the back office. Sunday we continued with the carpeting in the reception area and then hung the red shag carpeting on the wall. It was amazing, this place actually looked great!

When we finished, the office had been transformed from one that was sadly neglected, to one that screamed success and prosperity. However, we immediately became aware of another problem. Anyone who wanted to reach our office would have to walk down a long, drab, darkly lit hallway to its end. I feared that people would most likely flee before getting there. I now realized that the hallway was in even worse shape than our original office space.

I thought about this for a few minutes and then suggested to Richard, "Let's come back again next weekend. With help from Pepe and a houseman, we can drop the ceiling in the hallway, put in better lighting, paint the walls, and even put in some carpeting." I think that I was so used to making improvements in the hotel, whenever I thought it necessary, that I did not give any thought to the fact that this was not my property and that I was planning to make drastic alterations to a building, without the owner's approval. Nevertheless, we forged ahead. This effort meant another weekend of work but we accomplished what we set out to do without any difficulty. And what an improvement it was! The hallway looked inviting and cheerful.

Monday morning I was back at the hotel and Richard was working in our new office. Suddenly, Richard's phone rang, uh-oh ... a call from the landlord.

Mr. Fishbein spoke to him in what seemed to be an angry tone and asked in his heavy Yiddish accent, "Who vas da cuntractor?"

To which Richard asked, "Why?"

The only response he got was a raised voice again asking, "**Who vas de cuntractor?**"

I couldn't believe what Richard did! He gave the landlord my private number in the hotel. At least, he immediately called me to give me a heads up.

It didn't take too long before I received the dreaded phone call, "Hello, are you de cuntractor?"

"Yes."

"Vats yur name?"

I told him my name was Tony Fasone.

" I understand you did de job for Mr. Fogel?"

"Yes," I said. "Why do you ask?"

"I vant you to give me an estimate to do de udder two hallvays and de six batrooms, but, sharpen yur pencil. I vant a good price."

He had to be kidding—I couldn't believe my ears! Here I was so frightened that he would sue us and instead he wanted us to do more hallways. I couldn't wait to call Richard and relate my conversation with the landlord.

"Herb, why not, you've got the craftsman. Just figure out what the supplies will cost, how much Pepe's and another handyman's salary will be, and then add something on the top for us."

"But who is going to do the plumbing?"

"Can't you do it, Herb?"

"Look, I've never installed urinals."

"Well, get a book."

I know it sounds ridiculous but it was both a daunting and a tempting challenge to take on. The very next evening Annette was raring to go. Again she joined me at Pergament. This time we priced out toilets, urinals and sinks ... blue for the men's bathrooms and pink for the women's. We already knew the cost of material for a hallway from doing ours. Then I compiled a list, added the costs and totaled it. To this sum I added 25%. I have no idea where that number came from, but it sounded right to me. Except for Pepe and a handyman, I did not add in a cost for labor. I didn't think to charge for Richard's, Annette's or my labor and even if I did, what would I charge? I then returned Mr. Fishbein's call.

"Hello, Mr. Fishbein, this is Tony Fasone. My estimator surveyed your building and calculated the cost of the job."

"Did ya shapen yur pencil?"

I said, "Absolutely," and proceeded to tell him what the total cost of the job would be.

As I blurted out the sum I was sure he would scoff or bargain, but no, his response was, "Ven can ya start?"

"Mr. Fishbein, I'm finishing up a job on West 73rd Street and can start your building in ten days."

"Vunderful!"

I still had trepidations, but the challenge was pulling me like a vortex. The half- a-doctor was now moonlighting in the construction business.

During all the weekends of work, the landlord never met *Tony*, because Pepe was instructed to be a buffer.

Whenever Mr. Fishbein tried to go into a bathroom to observe, Pepe would yell,

"Hey man, the plumber's in there. You can't go in now."

The plumbing was definitely a learning experience, but notwithstanding the problems, we finally finished the job. We did it ... and all the halls and bathrooms looked great. I must say, I was proud of all we had accomplished and the office building was a pleasure to enter.

I received a call from Mr. Fishbein, complimenting and thanking me for the job and asking for the invoice. I prepared one using a form statement with Tony Fasone, Contractor typed on top followed by a P.O. Box number address and my private hotel phone number. Mr. Fishbein paid promptly.

The next few weeks unfolded in an unbelievable fashion for Tony Fasone, the contractor. In Mr. Fishbein's building there were offices as well as showrooms. Soon Tony was getting calls asking for estimates to upgrade and to renovate showrooms. One was a famous leather goods manufacturer, another a lingerie manufacturer, and a third was a cosmetic related business. I was hysterical with laughter. It was flattering to receive those calls, but I certainly knew my limitations.

Richard came up with a solution, "Sub it out to a real contractor."

We did; we also used him to help us with *real* estimates. Additionally, I used one of our hotel resident F.I.T. students to come up with a truly, modern, avante garde design for the leather goods company. This design was shipped to their corporate headquarters in Texas for review. Unbelievably, it was accepted with praise, and the requisite authorization order to begin the work followed quickly. In fact, we got all three jobs!

Tony, the contractor's name, was being bandied about in the Murray Hill community. One day, Tony received a call from the owner of two brownstone buildings on East 36th Street. He offered Tony a fifty percent ownership of the two buildings. Tony's investment would be the cost of renovating them. Everything was spinning too fast and getting out of control. Here I was running a hotel, trying to learn the agency/search business, and at the same time renovating showrooms. I had to make a choice. Annette kept encouraging me to go into the construction business ... she truly believed that I seemed happiest doing this kind of work. Even when I was working as a pharmacist, way back when, I was happiest when I was building shelves and showcases. However, I chose to put Tony out of the business. In retrospect, the brownstone deal might very well have been the better choice.

After having Tony exit the burgeoning construction business, the agency became my primary focus. Richard and I recruited and hired a real employment agency professional whom Richard closely observed and learned from. Not only did he bring in revenue but more importantly, he had the understanding and expertise to operate this type of business. Because of my hotel responsibilities, I could not devote any meaningful time to the agency effort. To compensate for this, Annette commuted daily from Rockland County to Manhattan, to work in my place. Part of her job was to scour the newspapers searching for companies that needed clerical help. Then using the assumed name of Angela Green, she would initiate calls to these companies, implying that she could provide the perfect person to fill their employment needs. If the company would be willing to set up an interview, she would then have to go through our list of possible applicants and, hopefully, find someone suitable to send out on the interview. Annette hated this job with a passion. Not only did she find it difficult to make cold calls, but also fabricating lies was an anathema to her. I recognized that a life changing decision had to be made soon. Both of us knew without saying it, that my days at the hotel were coming to an end.

I had been working as an innkeeper for the past fifteen years, I had two teenage daughters, a ten-year-old son, a loving wife, and a beautiful home in the suburbs ... life was good! At least on the surface it appeared so. But deep down, I felt like something was missing. Everything at the hotel had become predictable and routine. Even the robberies, suicides, and the expected/unexpected insanities from the asylum guests were becoming stale.

What had become apparent was the lack of a challenge. A new investment hotel property with management responsibilities would suffice, but given the economic climate, I knew that was not in the cards. I also knew that once I left the hotel, there would be no returning. It was a quandary that brought many sleepless nights. Richard was a very dynamic person who was reaching for the sky and as I had previously noted, his enthusiasm was infectious. The embryonic agency/ search business at its current stage would not enable my family to continue to enjoy the quality of life, which we now accepted as normal. But let's face it ... that was my challenge!

I knew that Mom would now be devastated if I LEFT the hotel. She enjoyed the daily banter and interchange with me, and I in turn enjoyed seeing and sharing time with her. I hoped that she would visit me often in my new office that was, as I said before, only two blocks away. I would certainly stop by to see her. Additionally, I was sure that Mom would be concerned about the financial uncertainty looming before me. Ironically, I did not realize that in the very near future, technology would make her position obsolete and force her into retirement.

My father-in-law had joined me at The Roger Williams Hotel a few years ago, when his management responsibilities at the restaurant ended with its sale. At that point my charter became the front desk, marketing and business development plus assisting with any heavy-duty maintenance activities. Pierre went back to being Hymie and assumed the responsibilities for bookkeeping, accounts payable and purchasing. So after I had managed the hotel for fifteen years, and without any regrets, I left the hotel and turned total management responsibility over to the capable hands of my father-in-law. Annette happily retired and I enthusiastically, though with some trepidation, replaced her at *The Madison Group*.

EPILOGUE

The original Investment Group continued to operate The Roger Williams Hotel until the conclusion of our thirty-five year lease in 1996. At that time, a new group acquired the hotel, changed its name to Hotel Roger Williams, and invested millions of dollars in renovations. They moved the entrance from East 3lst Street to Madison Avenue and made other innovative architectural changes. It is now an exclusive, sophisticated hotel offering amenities that I could have only dreamed of.

* * *

During my fifteen-year tenure, I was continually challenged with a particularly difficult painting problem. The weight of thirty years of paint layers was causing our ceilings to peel. Painting suppliers suggested burning the paint off the ceilings. Following their suggestions, I purchased a propane tank and tried the procedure myself. It was a tedious process but it worked. I then gave this responsibility to Ernie. Being the entrepreneur that he was, he decided to moonlight and use this newly acquired skill to paying customers in his neighborhood. About five years after I left the hotel, on one such contracting job, he accidentally set the draperies on fire. Sadly, Ernie perished in the blaze.

Richard Fogel and I worked together for ten years. After the first three years, our business-model changed from a contingency agency to a retainership executive search firm. Richard ultimately transitioned from executive search management to mergers and acquisitions, and private investment equity.

Paul Gold went on to write many successful books about sports. He became one of the country's most renowned sports authors.

After ten years with Richard, I along with Rosemary Kissel, a third partner at the Madison Group, left to form Eastbourne Associates. Eastbourne Associates evolved into a thriving executive search firm that successfully resolved search-consulting assignments both domestically as well as internationally. Annette came out of retirement, joining Eastbourne Associates as Director of Research. She thoroughly enjoyed working with Rosemary and me. We spent nineteen wonderful years together, always looking forward to the beginning of each new business day.